Rooted in the Faith

I0806853

ROOTED IN THE FAITH

Preparation for Church Membership

CHARLES P. ARAND

CONCORDIA PUBLISHING HOUSE • SAINT LOUIS

3558 S. Jefferson Ave., St. Louis, MO 63118-3968
1-800-325-3040 • www.cph.org

Manufactured in the United States of America

1 2 3 4 5 6 7 8 9 10   19 18 17 16 15 14 13 12 11 10

CONTENTS

Introduction

God makes promises. Faith clings to those promises. In a nutshell, therein lies the heart of the Christian faith and the Christian life. God promises to include us in the new creation. He promises to make us new creatures—beginning with our Baptism. Faith embraces those promises, for God is faithful. He sent His Son into the world to reclaim His creation. With His death, Jesus absorbed and removed the curse under which we and the rest of creation lay. With His resurrection, Jesus ushered in the new creation amid the old creation. By giving us faith, the Holy Spirit has made us a part of that new creation. That faith is like a seed that needs to be nurtured so that it may sprout and grow into full maturity. Faith is nurtured and strengthened by the Gospel promises. We find those promises embedded within the magnificent story of God.

Picture a tree nursery for a moment. Seeds are planted in pots of soil. The pots are placed in a greenhouse where they receive water and light. They are kept warm. Soon, the seeds come alive, germinate, and sprout from the soil. They draw on the rich, organic nutrients within the soil. So faith springs to life from the Gospel nutrients within the soil of God's story. Still fragile, the tender seedlings grow inch by inch and become stronger by the day. After awhile, the seedlings are moved outside the greenhouse. There they continue to grow in the pot along with other seedlings beneath the blue sky and bright sun.

Once the seedlings grow tall enough and strong enough, they are planted in the ground among other trees in a grove or perhaps a new forest. There they continue to grow among the other trees. There they continue to draw upon the rich nutrients in the soil. There they grow and weather the changing seasons: fall, winter, spring, and summer. There they may experience drought, rain, and wind. But as they grow along with the other trees, they form a community of trees, a forest. As part of a forest, they provide food and shelter for countless numbers of other creatures. As part of a forest, they prevent erosion, purify groundwater, and provide wind barriers.

© Maurice van der Velden / iStockphoto.com

This picture of a seed growing into a tree provides a snapshot of the Christian life. As we grow in faith, we go through a number of transitions or milestones. With Baptism, the seed of faith is planted within the soil of God's Word where the Gospel brings it to life and nourishes it. But that seedling needs to be nurtured and cultivated within the protective arms of the nursery so that it is not beaten down by the storms that blow its way. So it is for children and for adults who are new to the faith. We need the milk of the Word. Our roots in the faith need the rich nutrients of the Gospel. And so we receive instruction in the basics of the faith and receive the Gospel through the Service of the Word.

As we grow and become stronger, we encounter another milestone: confirmation. In some ways, it marks our transition from the greenhouse to joining the other trees in the grove. There with the congregation we continue to grow strong in order to bear fruit within the world. We join others in receiving the Lord's Supper. And we continue to draw on the riches of the Gospel. But now our roots stretch and expand so as to draw on the Gospel in all the stories and teachings of God's Word. We draw on those riches in order to become the human creatures that God has reclaimed us to be in the midst of all the seasons of life.

In this little book, we will explore that milestone in which we move from being baptized and rooted in the basics of the faith to living out those basics within all the areas and seasons of life. We will begin by looking at the shape of our life of faith as set forth in Luther's catechism. These are the basics, the richest of nutrients that we receive through teaching in connection with Baptism. These basics provide the structure for our lives, the DNA of our faith. We will continue by taking a look at the Rite of Confirmation, and the Rite of Reception of Members by Transfer or Profession of Faith, and see how our confession is made and witnessed in the congregation. Finally, we will explore how the basics of the faith (as set forth in Luther's catechism) help guide us throughout our lives as we read the Scriptures, worship as a community, engage in daily prayer, and tell others about Jesus. It's a marvelous journey!

Rooted in the Faith—Growing in Faith

Introduction

In the Rites of Confirmation and the Reception of Members, the uninitiated are asked whether they intend to remain faithful to Christ and to His Word until they fall asleep in Jesus. This is no easy task. Satan works hard to undermine faith in Christ. Satan seeks to lead Christians away from faith through false teachings. He tries to lead us away through persecutions. He tries to destroy our faith through the stresses of everyday life. He may even try to lead us away from faith with promises of an easier life that in the end prove to be little more than an illusion.

The apostle Paul warned the Christians of his day that followers of Christ would face various challenges to their faith. For this reason God has given His Church apostles and teachers in order that we might be built up in the faith, "so that we may no longer be children, tossed to and fro by the waves and carried about by every wind of doctrine, by human cunning, by craftiness in deceitful schemes" (Ephesians 4:14). Paul had seen firsthand how false teachings had misled the Galatians and the Corinthians.

The Early Church encountered not only many false teachings that threatened the faith but also a hostile culture and government. By the fourth century, the Church had gone through several severe persecutions during which many people had fallen away from the faith. Some pastors even renounced the faith by surrendering their Bibles. In the sixteenth century, Martin Luther discovered that the Roman Catholic Church itself had promoted superstitious views of God so that people falsely believed they could be saved by their own works. In addition, laypeople prayed to and relied upon the saints to plead their case with God.

In each of these situations, Paul, the Early Church, and Luther all emphasized the importance of growing strong in the faith. This involved two aspects. First, Christians need to grow in *the faith*. Christians need to become more and more familiar with the biblical teaching of the Gospel. Second, as Christians internalize the teachings of Scripture, they grow in *faith*. That is, they grow in the conviction that God's promises are true and that God will hold them firmly in His hands.

Picturing Faith in Christ

Consider a tree. After all, the Bible delights in drawing upon images from God's creation. For the inspired authors of the Bible, the natural world gives us direct contact with God's handiwork. So consider a sapling that grows into a mighty oak tree. As it sinks its roots into the ground and draws upon the nutrients in the soil, the tree grows in height and stature. It also bears much fruit. In addition, as the tree's roots grow deeper, the soil firmly anchors the tree so that it becomes capable of withstanding strong winds and storms.

We might think of our faith in Christ like that tree. Our faith starts out as a sapling—small and seemingly weak. But our faith sinks its roots into *the faith*, that is, the Scriptures, the Word of God. From that Word faith draws the water and nutrients necessary for its life and growth. It becomes more active in producing the fruits of faith. The deeper that our faith sinks its roots into the soil of *the faith*, the stronger and sturdier it grows within the world. Anchored deeply in the Word, our faith is better prepared to weather the storms of false teachings, persecutions, and trials that blow our way.

The Catechism: An Outline of the Faith

Paul encouraged people to cling to the faith that had been handed down to them. In the fourth century, the Church developed a catechetical (instruction in the basics) process that lasted from one to three years so that people would be strengthened against falling away during the next wave of persecutions. In that same spirit, Luther wrote both his Small and Large Catechisms so that people would be held firm in the basics of Scripture. They would be able to defend themselves against false teaching. The catechism should be seen as an outline that sets forth the basics of the faith. We can divide it into several sections.

The first section deals with the Ten Commandments, the Apostles' Creed, and the Lord's Prayer. Luther describes these as the heart of the Church's teaching. We might think of them as the humus in the soil. Humus is organic material that provides structure for the soil and at the same time supplies the nutrients that the roots of a tree need. In a similar way, the Ten Commandments, the Apostles' Creed, and the Lord's Prayer provide the structure for all the teachings of Scripture (the soil in which we sink our roots). They both summarize

Scripture and organize it for us. Together these three parts set forth our need for faith, the gift of faith, and the battle cry of faith.

The second section in Luther's catechism deals with Baptism, Absolution, and the Lord's Supper. The Church has referred to these as Sacraments or Means of Grace. If the Ten Commandments, the Apostles' Creed, and the Lord's Prayer are the humus that provides structure for the soil of God's Word, then Baptism, Absolution, and the Lord's Supper are the nutrients from the humus that awaken, nourish, and strengthen our faith. They deliver to us the Gospel of Christ that alone awakens faith in Jesus Christ. Together they sustain our faith from cradle to grave.

The third section in the catechism provides guidance for praying and living out our callings (or walks of life) within the world. These are the ways by which we exercise our faith. As we draw upon the nourishment provided by the Means of Grace, faith grows and expresses itself within the wider world by the way we live. And so the catechism provides morning, evening, and dinner prayers that Christians may use on a daily basis. The chart on Christian callings provides examples from Scripture concerning how we can live within our various walks of life.

Remarkably, Luther once admitted that he could not master the catechism as he wished. Instead, like a child, he had to remain a student of the catechism and was glad to do so (Large Catechism, Preface, paragraphs 7–8). This may seem odd, given the fact that he wrote the catechism! But upon closer reflection it makes sense. Like a tree, we never stop growing. In this life, faith sinks its roots ever deeper into the soil and continues to grow up within the world in the maturity of faith to which God has called us.

The following overview will explore the topics as they are presented in Luther's Small Catechism. Readers might want to follow along in their catechism as the overview begins.

THE TEN COMMANDMENTS

Dr. Luther would instruct us to begin with the Ten Commandments because they sketch out the shape of human life as God created it. They provide a blueprint for the life of faith. In the Ten Commandments we get a picture of what God wanted our lives to look like when He created us. They are the design specifications for how we are to live with God and one another within creation.

In his Large Catechism, Luther made the insightful observation that no one can live without faith. We are creatures, and as creatures we cannot live without depending upon someone or something. We depend upon the air that we breathe, the water we drink, and the food we eat. Take these away and we die. So the question we face is not "Will we have faith?" The question instead is "Where will we put our faith?" In what or in whom will we put our faith? The First Commandment, "You shall have no other gods," calls upon us to place our faith in the Creator and not in any part of creation.

Luther believed that we must remain students of the First Commandment for our entire life. "Therefore, however long we live, we shall always have our hands full if we remain pupils of the first commandment and of faith throughout all work and sufferings, and never cease to learn" ("Treatise on Good Works," LW 44:61).

The other commandments are closely connected to the First. In fact, they are so closely connected that it would be proper to think of them as nine commentaries on the First Commandment. Or we could say that the First Commandment is lived out in nine different ways. Trust in God is the foundation for keeping the rest of the commandments. This is why Luther opens every explanation with the words: "We should fear and love God so that..." Breaking any commandment reflects a lack of trust in God.

© Benjamin Goode / iStockphoto.com

The Second and Third Commandments deal with our relationship to God. We should not misuse God's name. When we have faith in God, then we call upon Him for what we need. When we expect nothing but good things from God, then we ask Him for our needs. If we do not expect anything from God, then we will not call upon Him. Or consider the Third Commandment: to "remember the Sabbath day by keeping it holy." Luther explains it in terms of gladly hearing and learning the Word of God. If we expect only good things from God, we will want to hear from Him and learn what He has to say to us. We will seek Him out and eagerly receive what He has to say.

The Fourth through Tenth Commandments deal with the different aspects of our relationships with our neighbors. In each one of them, trust in God becomes the prerequisite for loving and seeking the well-being of our neighbor. When we cling to God and rely upon Him, we rest safely in His hands. I do not have to worry about myself. The knowledge that we are secure in His hands frees us to look after our neighbor. Failure to trust in God results in harm to my neighbor. In nearly every instance, taking what belongs to my neighbor, speaking ill of my neighbor, or coveting things that belong to my neighbor betrays a lack of faith in God as the one who takes care of us.

Luther's presentation of the Commandments concludes with the threats and promises of God. With His threats, God warns us against placing our faith anywhere than in Him. This is not some kind of an ego trip on God's part. Instead, God is zealous for us because He knows that no one can provide for us what only He can provide. With His freely given and extravagant promises, He draws us to Himself. The Lord invites us to seek from Him all that we need and desire that we might love and trust Him and gladly do all that He asks.

THE APOSTLES' CREED

The stories of our lives shape our identities. They give rise to our values. They provide direction for our lives. Consider the story of the United States. The War of Independence, the Civil War, and the Civil Rights Movement have shaped who we are as a nation. Those stories have given rise to values that include personal freedoms, human rights, and democracy. These values in turn shape the way we live. When we evaluate whether or not to grant most-favored trade nation status to other countries, we consider their democratic reforms, human rights, and personal liberties.

Of course, a particular story played an instrumental role in shaping the identity of the Israelites in the Old Testament. This is the story of God's rescue of Israel from bondage in Egypt, their forty years of wandering in the wilderness, and the subsequent entry into Canaan. From that time on, the people of Israel told and retold the story (Deuteronomy 26:6–9; Psalm 136; Nehemiah 9). Whenever tempted to follow another god, they were to ask themselves, "Did this god deliver us out of Egypt?" If the answer was no, they were to avoid the temptation. This story gave rise to a way of living that included the exclusive worship of God.

The New Testament people believed that the story of Israel found its fulfillment and culmination in the appearance of Jesus Christ. Early on, the stories about Jesus were summarized by highlighting the key events of His life. Like all stories, they could be told in slightly different ways. But the events were the same. They included something of His origin and birth. They moved on to speak of His suffering and death. Then they culminated with a reference to Jesus' resurrection and exaltation to the right hand of God. These central events have shaped the Church Year, its worship, and its preaching.

Catechetical teaching planted Christians into the story of Jesus so that their roots could sink deeply into the account of God's relentless love in Jesus. This meant that more was involved than simply believing that the story of Christ was true. In order to grow in faith like a strong tree, Christians needed to firmly grasp with their roots and personally draw upon the promise of all God has done.

The First Article: Creation

> I believe that . . . God has made me and all creatures.

Imagine taking out a help wanted ad in the local newspaper—"Help Wanted: God." In other words, you are advertising for a job opening, namely, for someone to fill the position of being God. The ad continues, "Please submit your resume." Now the question arises, what would that resume look like? What qualifies one for the job of being God?

© Matthew Hertel / iStockphoto.com

Here is how the Bible would answer it: "If you created everything that exists, the job is yours. If you did not create everything that exists, you need not apply." In other words, the act of creation defines God. This is especially prominent in Isaiah 40–46 and continues into the New Testament (1 Corinthians 8). In the Large Catechism, Luther suggests that when someone asks, "Who or what is your God?" we should answer: "This is my God: first, the Father, who has created heaven and earth. Besides this One only, I regard nothing else as God. For there is no one else who could create heaven and earth" (Large Catechism II 11).

The conviction that God is the Creator provides the basis for the radical character of the biblical and creedal view of the world. To confess that God has created heaven and earth indicates that God created everything. You might say that He has created everything from A to Z! (See Genesis 1; Psalms 121, 134, 136, 146; Isaiah 40:18–23; 1 Timothy 6:13; Revelation 4:11; 10:6; 14:7.) The Small Catechism elegantly captures this thought when it states, "God has made me and ALL creatures."

If God created everything out of nothing, then everything that is not God must be a creature. This radical distinction between the Creator and the creature is the framework for our view of the world. The distinction between the Creator and the creature is greater than the distinction between any two creatures within the world! Creation provides the basis for the First Commandment. Do not confuse the Creator with His creation.

It also says something important about us. We are creatures. This may not seem like an important point to make; in fact, it may seem downright mundane and ordinary. Yet for Luther, there is no greater title or honor that a person can have than to be called a creature of God. It is a greater thing to be called a creature than to be called a president or a CEO. It is such a great thing to be a creature because it means that you are the personal handiwork of God. And so Luther urges, "Learn to think of yourself as a creature and you will be a greater professor than all the professors of the university!"[1] Luther wants to impress upon the hearer that God's creating activity determines who I am. I am a creature of God! As a creature of God, I relate to God as a receiver, as one who is completely dependent upon God. To see ourselves as creatures is to recognize that God is the exclusive giver of our lives and all that we need for our lives. (See LW 43:210.)

But I am not the only creature that God has made. God has created me together with other creatures. The word *together* establishes solidarity between me and all of God's other creatures. By speaking of animals and birds as "creatures," Luther shows that he does not regard creation as little more than a stockpile of raw materials. He sees creation in personal terms. The trees and fruits of the earth, the sun and moon, are all fellow creatures! Luther's approach reflects the way in which the Psalms also speak, especially when the Psalms describe how the entire creation praises its creator (Psalm 148).

All the other creatures, the entire creation, are gifts from God. They help sustain our lives. Through other creatures God nourishes us and protects us. Luther describes them as masks of God. We might use another image. Creatures are gloves on God's hands. God deals with us through His creation. He has blessed the earth to bring forth its fruits. Through cows He provides milk and butter. Through chickens He provides eggs and meat. Through trees He provides oxygen. Through wetlands He purifies our water. We are not to seek our needs from God apart from His servants through whom He provides for us. But we must distinguish the hand from the glove, the source from the means. Faith perceives the hand behind the gift. Unbelief stops at the gift and assumes that it is the source.

---

1. *Katechismuspredigten* (1528), in *D. Martin Luthers Werke: Kritische Gesamtausgabe* (Weimar: H. Böhlau, 1910), 30/1:88.22ff.

The catechism then takes us on a wondrous journey of discovery with the First Article of the Apostles' Creed. So we begin at the point where we most directly encounter God's creative work, namely, our own person. We begin by saying that God has given me body and soul, along with what they entail. In other words, God has given me a body made up of eyes, ears, and all my members. Luther's list is simply to get us thinking about all that makes us what we are. He describes my soul in terms of reason and all my senses. God has also given me imagination, intelligence, sight, hearing, and so on.

Luther's approach may appear to be too "human centered." It might sound as if the entire universe exists for no other purpose than to serve our needs. But we need to remember that Luther's intention is not to map out the universe. Nor is it to suggest that every creature exists only to serve our needs. He knew well enough from the Book of Job that everything is not just about us (Job 38–40)!

The catechism has a more modest pedagogical purpose of strengthening faith in God's good provision. To that end Luther takes us by the hand and leads us out into the world in order to perceive the world as a gift of God, beginning with what we might call the basic necessities of life such as food and drink, clothing and shoes, spouse and children, house and home, field and cattle. Finally, the catechism leads us into the wider world in order to perceive the entire world as a gift of God. In the Large Catechism, Luther specifically mentions weather, government, the sun, moon, and stars, and so on.

The goal of stressing God as Creator and humans as creatures is to form our faith in such a way that we look to God alone for every need in life. Luther encourages people to consider God as the exclusive giver of their creaturely existence. In other words, the First Article seeks to arouse and strengthen faith in God's creaturely and providential care. The First Article enables the Christian to pray the refrain in the morning and evening prayers: "For into Your hands I commend myself, my body and soul, and all things."

SECOND ARTICLE: REDEMPTION

I believe that . . . Jesus is [has become] My Lord.

Heroes are individuals who save people by means of extraordinary action in which they risk their lives. Following 9/11 we hailed the firefighters of the New York Fire Department as heroes when they entered the Twin Towers in order to rescue those trapped on floors engulfed by flames. Soldiers who give their lives for their country are rightly hailed as heroes. A hero gives us someone whom we can admire and from whom to draw inspiration.

The image of a hero can help us understand what the catechism means when we affirm that Jesus has become our Lord. The image of a lord evokes times gone by when we lived in a world of lords and ladies, dukes and duchesses. Those of a higher station might be addressed as "my lord." But the notion of a hero as a rescuer comes a little closer to what the catechism means by "lord." Luther suggests that "Lord" simply means the same as "redeemer," that is, "rescuer." Of course, the comparison of Lord and hero can only go so far. Jesus as Lord differs in two significant ways.

First, a hero is generally recognized as an individual who through extraordinary effort accomplished the rescue of someone who otherwise might have died. In the Small Catechism, Jesus is described as true God and true man. In doing so, Luther simply draws upon the teachings of the Nicene Creed and the ecumenical councils of the Early Church. Jesus is both begotten of the Father and born of the Virgin Mary. It is perhaps worth noting that the language of Lord in the New Testament has connotations of the divine. It is often used as a title for God. In fact, the most common confession of the Christians in the New Testament was "Jesus is Lord." But the catechism develops this further. Not only do we say that "Jesus is Lord," we say that "Jesus is *my* Lord!"

Second, when a firefighter saves a person from a burning building, the firefighter's responsibility toward that individual comes to an end. The individual returns to his family and goes about daily business. Of course, he remains grateful to the firefighter and may even remain in contact with the firefighter. But the firefighter has no further responsibility for the rescued person. Such is not the case with Jesus. He rescues us from hopelessness and condemnation brought on by sin, death, and the power of the devil. But He rescued us in order that we may belong to Him, live under Him, and serve Him.

And so the Second Article tells the story of how Jesus rescued us and became our Lord. It is the most dramatic and compelling story ever told. The Large Catechism begins when God formed humans from the earth. The devil then came and misled Adam and Eve (and with them the entire human race) into sin and unbelief. Here there is both a sense of being deceived by Satan and at the same time willingly following the devil's advice. As a result, the human race found itself captive to sin, death, and the power of the devil. Satan had become the jailor and tyrant of the world. Human beings also now found themselves under the condemnation of God for their complicity. But all was not lost, for the Son of God had mercy upon us and in love came down from heaven and became incarnate as a human being.

At this point the Large Catechism tells the story in vivid colors. It paints the picture of a battlefield. On one side of the battlefield, lined up from horizon to horizon, is Satan with all of his minions and allies. We find ourselves as captives and POWs behind enemy lines. Sin, death, and the devil are our masters. Then the Son of God comes down to earth to reclaim His human creatures and His creation. He appears as our champion on the battlefield, like David facing Goliath. Satan becomes enraged as he recognizes that his domain is threatened. And so Satan strikes the first blow with the temptation of Jesus in the desert after His Baptism. Christ counters with His miracles, exorcisms, and preaching. The devil plotted the death of Jesus. Satan's allies killed Jesus and threw Him in the grave, but with His resurrection, Jesus left sin and death buried in the grave. He has become our Lord.

We can also perhaps think of a lord as an owner—one who owns that which is under his control. We can also think of a lord as one who rules, one who governs his property and controls that which belongs to him. To say that Jesus is Lord means that He has reclaimed His creatures for Himself. To say that Jesus is my Lord is to say that I belong to Jesus. I "belong to Him." I am under His jurisdiction and gracious rule. I "live under Him in His kingdom." As Lord or King, Jesus has taken on the responsibility of providing for us and protecting us from all harm.

The Small Catechism provides us with important insight about how to live both now and in the new creation. We declare that Jesus rose from the dead that

"I might be His own." He has given me a new identity. I am now a creature who has been adopted as a child of God. I am identified with Him. He defines who I am. At the same time, I live out this new identity by what I do. He is my Lord. I belong to Him. And so I "serve Him in everlasting righteousness, innocence, and blessedness." This serving is not a case of exchanging one tyrant for another. It simply means that now I can live out my life as He had created us to do for the sake of His creation.

THIRD ARTICLE: SANCTIFICATION

I believe that . . . the Holy Spirit has called me by the Gospel.

The Holy Spirit is usually identified with the work of sanctification, the work of making one holy. In large part, this is the result of one of Luther's chief insights in both of his catechisms. When we think of the Holy Spirit, we cannot but help conclude that the word *holy* describes a particular characteristic of the Spirit. In other words, the Spirit is holy. This is certainly true. The Spirit is morally pure and completely set apart from us. And yet there is more: The catechism also suggests that the Holy Spirit is called holy because the word *holy* describes what the Holy Spirit does for us and to us. That is to say, the Spirit makes us holy! This is simply another way of saying that the Holy Spirit sanctifies us.

At this point, we might want to clarify what the word *sanctification* means. Many people see it primarily as a way to describe how Christians gradually get better and better in terms of morality—the moral improvement within their lives and the progress that they make in doing good works. As they progress in their moral improvement, they begin living less and less sinful lives. While this is a good start, the danger exists that it might suggest we can reach a point where we no longer need Jesus as Savior. In other words, if I can rid myself of sinful habits, then I no longer need forgiveness (which means I no longer need Jesus). Indeed, non-Christians might see this as part of a self-righteous attitude on the part of many Christians.

In the catechisms, Luther has a helpful way of addressing what it means to be made holy. In the course of his discussion, he describes sanctification from two perspectives.

First, Luther contends in his Large Catechism that the Holy Spirit makes us holy by bringing us to the Lord Jesus to receive His blessings of forgiveness, salvation, and life everlasting. The Small Catechism opens the Explanation of the Third Article by stating that "I cannot by my own reason or strength believe in Jesus Christ, my Lord, or come to Him; but the Holy Spirit has called me to faith by the Gospel, enlightened me with His gifts, sanctified and kept me in the true faith." In other words, the Spirit sanctifies us by bringing us to Jesus.

This might sound like the catechisms are really talking about what we call justification—not sanctification. But for Luther, the moment that the Spirit creates faith to receive the gifts that Christ won for us on the cross, He has made us holy. In other words, in God's eyes, I really am holy! After all, if we have received the forgiveness of sins, then there are no more sins that can condemn us. Every time we receive the forgiveness of sins, our sins are removed as far as the east is from the west. It is for this reason that Paul can refer to the people for whom he wrote his letters as saints. They are the saints at Ephesus or the saints at Philippi. Paul could even refer to the people at Corinth, with all the problems and dissensions that they exhibited, as saints in Jesus Christ.

Second, Luther also refers to the Spirit's work of sanctification in the more traditional manner of "progressive holiness." But even here, he does not describe it primarily in terms of reforming our external behavior. Luther's focus is really on faith. He anticipates that the Christian will grow in the confidence of God's grace in Jesus Christ. And as faith grows, like a tree, the fruits of faith will increase as a matter of course. In fact, one time Luther suggested that faith is so dynamic that before one asks what good works should be done, faith will already have done them! But he notes that in this life we will never be made fully holy. For faith is always under attack by the devil, temptations, and trials.

The remaining list of items in the Third Article describes the means by which the Spirit sanctifies us. He sanctifies us by means of the "holy Christian church, the communion of saints, the forgiveness of sins, the resurrection of the body, and the life everlasting." Through these events the Spirit both brings us to faith and destroys sin within our lives until we are completely rid of all sin with the resurrection of the body.

In the Small Catechism it is worth noting that we move from confessing how the Spirit brings us to Christ to learning about how the Spirit brings and gathers the entire Church to Jesus and keeps it with Him. He brings me to faith just as "He calls, gathers, enlightens, and sanctifies the whole Christian church on earth." So the Spirit brings me to faith in the same way that He brings everyone else to faith, namely, through someone sharing the Gospel.

This is another way of saying that no one comes to faith without contact with the Church. Someone shares the Gospel with us, puts it in our hands, or brings us to Baptism. So the very moment that we came to faith, we were also gathered into the Church. That is what Church means for Luther. It is a gathering of believers. We could say that it is a group of believers who congregate (a congregation) together around the Gospel and are bound to one another by the promise of the Gospel. This is what they share in common.

In this Christian Church, we receive the one thing that cannot be found in any other community within the world. The Small Catechism says, "In this Christian church [the Spirit] daily and richly forgives all my sins and the sins of all believers." He does this through the proclamation of the Gospel, Baptism, Absolution, and the Lord's Supper. The task of forgiving sins is the unique task that Christ gave His Church. This is not to say that the Church doesn't do other things as part of the new creation (like looking after people's physical needs and well-being), but it all begins here with the forgiveness of sins. For with the forgiveness of sins, the new creation breaks into the world. It brings with it the resurrection of the body when Christ returns in glory.

The Lord's Prayer

Satan is defeated, but he has not yet been banished forever. The world, the flesh, and the devil still remain active until Christ returns in glory. Having failed to prevent Christ from accomplishing redemption, Satan now devotes himself to preventing us from enjoying the gifts of redemption. Satan works hard to convince us that Christ's forgiveness does not apply to us. In this way he seeks to deprive us of faith and the gifts of Christ. So now we find ourselves on the front line of the battle between God and Satan. Christ does not rescue us in order to let us slide back under those jailers and tyrants. In this battle, prayer becomes one of our most important weapons. In prayer we turn our back on Satan and turn to God.

In the Large Catechism, Luther identifies two reasons for prayer. The first is that it is God's command. God does not want to hear from us only when we have a moment to spare. God insists that we pray because no one else can help us in our battle with unbelief. It is as if God were to say, "Pray! Ask Me for help. I want to help you." Second, we have God's promise to hear our prayers. For Luther, the promise is the basis for praying with confidence. To put it in the words of the Small Catechism, it is so that "with all boldness and confidence we may ask [God] as dear children ask their dear father."

© iStockphoto.com

We regard the Lord's Prayer as an ideal model for prayer because it is the very prayer that our Lord gave us. In it, He teaches what we need. If left to ourselves, we might ask only for those things that pertained to our daily bread (physical needs). But the Lord's Prayer helps us to see all of our needs and to open wide our arms to receive all that God wishes to give us. And so Jesus gives us seven requests to make. These requests make it clear that in this life we will always address God out of need.

It has been common to divide the Lord's Prayer into two sets of petitions. The first three petitions all deal with God: His name, His kingdom, and His will. These are called the "Thy" petitions. The next four petitions deal with our needs: daily bread, forgiveness, protection from temptation, and deliverance from evil. These are called the "our" petitions. Biblical scholars have suggested a variety of ways to think about the sequence of these two groups. For example, one could argue that we first pray for God, and then we pray for ourselves. Another way to look at it is to say that we first pray for eternal gifts, and then we pray for those things we need in the meantime.

The requests or petitions of the Lord's Prayer might be summarized much as the catechism explains it: in terms of faith. In other words, the one need we have above all other needs and for which we pray is for faith—faith to receive the blessings of God that Christ acquired for us upon the cross. Thus we pray for faith. At the same time, we pray for protection against unbelief and against Satan's efforts to deceive us. For this reason, the explanations that appear in the catechism similarly start with: "God's name is certainly holy in itself, but we pray in this petition that it may be kept holy among us also." In other words, we pray that we may receive in faith and with thanks all these gifts that God has promised.

We look forward to the second and final invasion of our Lord into this world, at which time He will finally banish sin, death, and the devil so that they will no longer have any access to us. Christ's defeat of the devil culminates in the last judgment; "Deliver us from evil" (Seventh Petition).

Baptism

Thus far we have considered the soil of the faith into which we sink the roots of our faith. The deeper we sink our roots into the soil of God's Word, the stronger our faith and the better we are able to withstand the storms that assault us. As we sink our roots into the soil, we draw upon the rich nutrients of the Gospel. Gardeners often speak of three essential nutrients required to make plants healthy, namely, nitrogen, phosphorous, and potassium. By analogy, we might say that we now turn to the three essential nutrients (or delivery systems) that faith needs, namely, Baptism, Absolution, and the Lord's Supper. These three provide the Gospel in three different forms for the health and strengthening of faith.

The Christian life begins with Baptism. Baptism transfers us from the kingdom of Satan to the kingdom of Christ. What Christ accomplished on the cross is now delivered to us in Baptism.

Baptism consists of God's command, God's promise, and water. The **command** is another way of speaking about the establishment of Baptism. Here the catechism points to Matthew 28:19, the Great Commission, where Christ said to go and make disciples and to baptize them. The **promise** is tied to the name of God. In Matthew 28, Jesus said to baptize in the name of the Father, the Son, and the Holy Spirit, and that name becomes a promise. In placing His name upon us, God promises to be our heavenly Father, to keep us safe in Jesus Christ, and to strengthen us by means of the Holy Spirit. In other words, we now belong to God. He is ours and we are His. Finally, Christ attaches His name to the **water**. The catechism describes it as water "combined with God's Word." It is stronger than that. The point is that here in Baptism water encloses the Word or the Word encloses the water. It can go in either direction.

We turn again to Matthew 28:19 to understand what Baptism accomplishes. Jesus says to go "and make disciples of all nations." We might think of nations as countries other than our own. But in Jesus' day, the word *nations* meant primarily the pagans, that is, those who were outside the covenant that God had established with Israel. Today, we would equate pagans with unbelievers or non-Christians. Baptism is intended for unbelievers. It is how non-Christians become Christians. In this regard, we might think of Baptism as the missionary sacrament of the Church.

© Paul Hart / iStockphoto.com

It is for this reason that the Large Catechism relies heavily on passages from John 3 and Titus 3. In the former, Baptism is described in terms of a new birth. It is a new start on life that is produced by God. Just as a mother gives birth to a baby (without any cooperation on the part of the baby), so the Spirit gives birth to new Christians through the water of Baptism. Similarly, Titus speaks of it in terms of a bath of regeneration. It is a bath that washes away the sins of the individual and gives that person a new life. This all happens by virtue of the promise of God that is encapsulated within the water that is applied to the baby or to the adult. For this reason, we exult in the water of Baptism. Many have suggested that we remind ourselves of Baptism when showering or washing or standing in the rain. Just as that water cleanses us, it reminds us of what Baptism did for us.

But Luther does not stop there. One of the most important parts of the catechism's treatment on Baptism can be found in the fourth question: "What does such baptizing with water indicate?" Here Luther explores the ongoing significance of Baptism for the entire life of the Christian, drawing upon Romans 6. There Paul declared that when we were baptized, we were joined to Christ. More significant, we were united with Christ in His death and united with Christ in His resurrection. Thus, in Baptism, we literally died to sin and rose from the dead to a new life in Christ.

From there Luther sees the entire life of the Christian as a daily Baptism. In other words, every day we live out our Baptism by dying and by rising. This has become the rhythm of the Christian life. Every day when you and I confess our sins, we in a sense die to those sins. We tell God, "Please take them away from me. I don't want them anymore. Get them out of my sight!" In turn, when we recall the promises of God or hear the words of Absolution, we are revived once again. Faith renews us and makes us alive. And so Luther in the Large Catechism can describe Baptism as the daily garment of the Christian. We live out our Baptism through the rhythm of dying and rising, Confession and Absolution, Law and Gospel.

Confession

Luther provides three questions about confession followed by a brief form or example of what it might look like. Some treat this as a separate section of the catechism (Fifth Chief Part) while others might regard it more as an appendix or extension to the section on Baptism. In either case, it follows nicely. We live out our Baptism by dying and rising, Confession and Absolution.

Luther's concern at this point was to remove the torturous conditions that had been placed on confession in the Middle Ages. People had been told that if they could not remember every single sin that they had ever committed, then those particular sins remained unforgiven. In other words, unconfessed sin was unforgiven sin. Luther wanted to shift people's attention to the purpose of going to confession, namely, to receive absolution! Thus, when you take a look at this little form or example of how to confess, it quickly becomes evident that Luther does not want Christians to beat themselves up through a torturous self-examination. Instead, he encourages them to confess the sins about which they are aware and then to receive the comfort of the forgiveness of sins.

© Zsolt Nyulaszi / iStockphoto.com

THE LORD'S SUPPER

If Baptism is how we became Christians, then the Lord's Supper, the Sacrament of the Altar, provides us with daily sustenance for life as we await the new creation. Like Baptism, three parts of the Lord's Supper stand out: Christ's commission, the promise, and the bread and wine. Jesus established the Lord's Supper for His followers on the evening before He died. Matthew, Mark, and Luke all record Jesus' words to eat and drink His body and His blood. This is the same body and blood that was given for us on the cross and that was raised from the dead. This is the same body and blood that acquired salvation for us. In other words, we receive the very body and blood that obtained the forgiveness of sins for us. In receiving that body and blood, we receive the salvation and forgiveness of sins that they purchased. And so God has provided yet another way for us to receive His forgiveness: in the bread and wine. As the water contains the triune name in Baptism, so the bread and wine of the Lord's Supper "contains" the body and blood of Jesus.

One issue that has divided Protestants more than any issue over the past five hundred years revolves around whether or not the body and blood of Christ are actually delivered to, and received by, Christians who eat the bread and drink the wine. Many say that it is impossible for God. Luther took God at His Word. The One who brought the entire universe into existence by simply speaking is the same God who speaks to us in the Sacrament, "This is My body and this is My blood." Faith lets God be God and thus takes Him at His Word. For this reason, Luther stresses that the Word is the key to the Sacrament of the Lord's Supper.

For just as the Word made water into a life-giving water, so the Word makes bread and wine the body and blood of Christ. Nothing less than the forgiveness of sins is at stake. To deny the body and blood ultimately denies the forgiveness of sins that they bring. The body and blood of Christ delivers the forgiveness of sins. Take these away and you take away the forgiveness of sins.

There was a time in the Middle Ages when people felt that they had to purify themselves in order to be worthy of the Lord's Supper. It was assumed that Christ, the pure and perfect Bridegroom, could not unite Himself with an impure and imperfect bride. Thus Christians needed to purify themselves with good works before receiving the Lord's Supper. For this reason, Luther asks the question, "Who receives this sacrament worthily?" He answers: "That person is truly worthy and well prepared who has faith in these words: 'Given and shed for you for the forgiveness of sins.' " In other words, faith makes one worthy. Faith receives the gifts of Christ, the very gifts that cleanse us and purify us. In faith, Christ takes on our sinfulness and our death while we receive His forgiveness and His life. Faith receives the body and blood that is the forgiveness of sins for us.

EXERCISE OF FAITH

In the final sections of the catechism, we turn to practices by which we exercise our faith. These practices include daily prayers and guidance for living within our callings.

Luther begins by providing samples of prayers for use in everyday life. These constituted a break with the past. The piety of the Middle Ages tied devotions and prayers to the monastic hours that occurred seven times a day. Luther chose to connect our prayers to the routine of everyday life. We have to get up in the morning and go to work. We have to eat. And we have to go to bed at night. Those provided the occasions for prayer. And so the catechism includes morning and evening prayers as well as prayers to use at mealtime.

A couple of characteristics stand out in Luther's selection of prayers. First, prayer is a response to the Word of God. Notice how he opens the meal prayer with a wonderful passage from Psalm 145. This passage reminds us of God's generosity and how He satisfies the needs of all of His creatures. God's goodness both invites us to ask for His blessing on the food that we are about to eat and to give Him thanks for taking care of our daily needs.

Second, prayer gives voice to faith. Luther's morning and evening prayers are good examples. Each of them concludes: "into Your hands I commend myself, my body and soul, and all things." Note the advice that Luther then gives: Go to work joyfully, knowing that God will bless the work of your hands. Or, in the evening, lay your head on your pillow and go to sleep. Do not lie there, tossing and turning, worrying about tomorrow. You have just put all things into God's hands.

In the next section, Luther provides a Table of Duties, a chart of Christian callings. This deals with how we should think about our walks of life. Part of the reason that Luther does this is that, during the Middle Ages, the only people who were considered to have "callings" were people who belonged to the religious orders, including monks, nuns, and priests. Luther's recovery of the biblical teaching on salvation carried the ramification that no one is closer to God than another because of the kind of life they live. In Christ, all people stand on an equal footing before God.

Luther wanted every Christian to see that he or she had been called by

God to serve others for the well-being of God's creation. Parents had a calling to take care of their children. Children were called by God to heed their parents. Magistrates were called to serve their people. Citizens were called to look after their community. In brief, the needs of our neighbor served as God's call to assist. In this way, Luther could speak of every God-pleasing walk of life in which Christians live as a "calling" from God. To assist them, Luther provides a collection of Bible passages that highlight the responsibilities Christians have within their various vocations.

RECEIVING NEW MEMBERS

CONFESSING THE FAITH ONCE DELIVERED TO THE SAINTS

Confirmation is the public rite of the Church that is preceded by a period of instruction designed to help baptized Christians identify with the life and mission of the Christian community.

Having been instructed in the Christian faith prior to admission to the Lord's Supper (1 Corinthians 11:28), the rite of Confirmation provides an opportunity for the individual Christian, relying on God's promise given in Holy Baptism, to make a personal public confession of the faith and a lifelong pledge of fidelity to Christ.[1]

In the same way, the public rite for receiving those who have been confirmed in a previous Lutheran congregation provides an individual the opportunity to join through public confession of the faith once delivered to the saints believed, taught, and confessed in this congregation.

1. *Lutheran Worship: Altar Book* (St. Louis: Concordia, 1982), 33.

Let us look at the confirmation service and the rite for receiving those who are making a profession of faith. The wording of the rite is located on the left side of the page; a brief commentary is on the right. It is good to familiarize yourself with the service so you can understand what will happen and can ask your pastor about any section that may not be clear to you.

Confirmation

Confirmation is a custom of the Church and not a sacrament. It links the catechumens to their Baptism, celebrates the reception of the Lord's Word among them, and welcomes them to the Lord's Table. Confirmation declares that a catechumen is a Christian who is baptized, confesses the faith, and is in communion with Christ and His Church. The reception of a catechumen to the Lord's Table assumes that ongoing catechesis is the way of life for the faithful Christian. This rite emphasizes God's work in Baptism, the gift of faith, and the benefits of the Lord's Supper for all who believe in Christ and the words of His testament.

[**Note:** In the case of adult Baptism, where instruction precedes the ministration of Holy Baptism, neither confirmation nor any other rite need be used, since this sacrament brings the individual into the full fellowship of the Church.]

The pastor addresses the catechumens.

P Beloved in the Lord, our Lord Jesus Christ said to His apostles: "All authority has been given to Me in heaven and on earth. Therefore go and make disciples of all nations, baptizing them in the name of the Father and of the Son and of the Holy Spirit, teaching them to observe all things that I have commanded you; and lo, I am with you always, even to the end of the age." You have been baptized and catechized in the Christian faith according to our Lord's bidding. Jesus said, "Whoever confesses Me before men, I will also confess before My Father who is in heaven. But whoever denies Me before men, I will also deny before My Father who is in heaven." Lift up your hearts, therefore, to the God of all grace and joyfully give answer to what I now ask you in the name of the Lord.

Matthew 28:18b–20 NKJV; Matthew 10:32–33 NKJV alt.

P Do you this day in the presence of God and of this congregation acknowledge the gifts that God gave you in your Baptism?

R *Yes, I do.*

ADDRESS TO THE CATECHUMENS

The Rite of Confirmation gives us the opportunity to declare ourselves disciples of Jesus! In Matthew 28, Jesus gave His disciples the commission to make other disciples. They were given the task of baptizing people and teaching them everything that the Lord has commanded. In the Rite of Confirmation we publicly celebrate the carrying out of these two activities. In the case of children, we baptize first and then teach them as they grow. In the case of adults, we teach first and then baptize. In these ways, Jesus makes disciples.

BAPTISMAL QUESTION

We confess that we are Jesus' disciples because we have received Christ's gifts in Baptism! When we were baptized, the Holy Spirit rescued us from the tyranny of Satan and placed us under the gracious care of Christ. He removed our unbelief and gave us faith. He raised us from death and gave us life. The next few questions ask us to confess this marvelous event: our rescue from Satan's realm of death and our transfer into Christ's realm of life.

P Do you renounce the devil?
R *Yes, I renounce him.*

P Do you renounce all his works?
R *Yes, I renounce them.*

P Do you renounce all his ways?
R *Yes, I renounce them.*

RENUNCIATION OF THE DEVIL

Discipleship begins by renouncing what we leave behind. So it was for the first disciples, and so it is for us. The rite opens with a rejection of our old master, Satan. It is a complete disavowal. We not only reject him, but we reject his methods of deception and his works of unbelief. Nothing makes Satan angrier than when we turn our backs on him. But we now cling to One who is much stronger than Satan. We have taken on a new name and live under the name of the Father, Son, and Holy Spirit.

P Do you believe in God, the Father Almighty?
R *Yes, I believe in God, the Father Almighty, maker of heaven and earth.*

CONFESSION OF GOD THE FATHER

Having renounced the devil, who has taken his place? To whom do we now cling? Luther suggested in his Large Catechism that we begin by answering: He is the one who "created heaven and earth!" (Large Catechism II 11). This is a way of saying that there is no other God. If God did not create everything that exists, then He is not God. This truth is the basis of the First Commandment's prohibition to have no other gods. We also confess that God is "almighty." He continues to actively rule over all things.

CONFESSION OF JESUS CHRIST

My God not only created me, but He also rescued me from Satan's clutches. The story is dramatic and remarkable. The Creator became a human creature. The Son of God, our Creator, then suffered and died for us. This last statement seemed so incredible that the creed hammers home the reality of His suffering with four drumbeats: "suffered, crucified, died, and buried." In this Jesus achieved His victory. His victory was announced with a victory parade. First, He went into the heart of enemy territory (hell); and then, upon being raised, He went to His disciples (on earth); and then He ascended to the realm of angels (heaven), where He took His place on the throne alongside the Father.

P Do you believe in Jesus Christ, His only Son, our Lord?
R *Yes, I believe in Jesus Christ, His only Son, our Lord, who was conceived by the Holy Spirit, born of the virgin Mary, suffered under Pontius Pilate, was crucified, died and was buried. He descended into hell. The third day He rose again from the dead. He ascended into heaven and sits at the right hand of God the Father Almighty. From thence He will come to judge the living and the dead.*

CONFESSION OF THE HOLY SPIRIT

Jesus does not leave us alone in this world. Upon ascending into heaven, the Father sent the Spirit into the world in order to bring people to Christ through the Gospel. By means of the Spirit we are enabled to cry out to God as Father (Galatians 4:1–7). The Spirit continues the work of Christ here on earth. Where Christ obtained salvation for us, the Spirit now delivers that salvation to us. He does so within the Church where He keeps us safe with Christ and brings us to everlasting life through the resurrection of the body.

P Do you believe in the Holy Spirit?
R *Yes, I believe in the Holy Spirit, the holy Christian Church, the communion of saints, the forgiveness of sins, the resurrection of the body, and the life everlasting.*

P Do you hold all the prophetic and apostolic Scriptures to be the inspired Word of God?
R *I do.*

Confession of the Word of God

As disciples we are students of God's Word. Thus we are asked to remain students of that Word. A disciple never stops growing in the Word. From the beginning, Christians have recognized that the Scriptures convey the very words of God Himself. God has spoken through the prophets in the Old Testament and the apostles in the New Testament. The Spirit inspired them to write down God's Word for the Church. When we read or hear the words of the prophets and apostles, we hear and read the Holy Spirit's own words. By speaking with us, God keeps us close to Himself.

P Do you confess the doctrine of the Evangelical Lutheran Church, drawn from the Scriptures, as you have learned to know it from the Small Catechism, to be faithful and true?
R *I do.*

Confession of the Teaching of the Lutheran Church

As disciples, we are not loners. We learn from others who in creeds and confessions have shared what they have learned. The Apostles' Creed summarizes the faith that Christians have treasured for centuries. In a similar way, the Small Catechism summarizes the Scriptures for those new to the faith. The Large Catechism helps pastors and mature Christians to plumb the depths of Scriptures' treasures. And so here we confess that the teachings of the Lutheran Church as summarized in the catechism correspond to the Bible's witness to Christ.

INTENTION TO LIVE A FAITHFUL LIFE

Thus far we have renounced our former master, the devil, and with him a life of unbelief. We then confessed our faith in the triune God by confessing all that the Father, Son, and Holy Spirit have done in our lives. We now look toward the future. How will we carry out our callings as people who live under the gracious lordship of Jesus Christ?

INTENTION TO USE THE MEANS OF GRACE

P Do you intend to hear the Word of God and receive the Lord's Supper faithfully?
R *I do, by the grace of God.*

The Holy Spirit made us disciples of Christ by means of the Gospel. By hearing the Word of God we enter into conversation with Christ whereby He comes and reassures us of His love and care. And that is not all. Jesus invites us to His table with the words, "Take eat; take drink." Here He gives us His very body and blood by which He obtained the forgiveness of sins for us. By means of this meal, Christ keeps us close to Himself until He returns in glory and raises us from the dead, at which time we will enjoy an eternal banquet in the new creation.

INTENTION TO LIVE BY THE WORD

P Do you intend to live according to the Word of God, and in faith, word, and deed to remain true to God, Father, Son, and Holy Spirit, even to death?
R *I do, by the grace of God.*

As disciples we will face many distractions in life. We will encounter temptations to turn away from Jesus. Our lives depend upon the Word of God. It nourishes us and keeps us with Christ. To deny the Word is to reject the one who speaks to us and keeps us close to Him. And so there is a connection between living according to the Word and living under the care of the Father, Son, and Holy Spirit.

P Do you intend to continue steadfast in this confession and Church and to suffer all, even death, rather than fall away from it?
R *I do, by the grace of God.*

INTENTION TO REMAIN FAITHFUL TO DEATH

The road that Jesus chose was not an easy one. It led Him to the cross for our salvation. Jesus calls upon us as His disciples to follow Him. When we renounced Satan and confessed Christ, we entered into a battle that will continue until Christ returns in glory. Satan will use the various struggles and trials of life to raise doubts about God's goodness. He will try and seduce us into idolizing the good things in life in order to draw us away from God. God has promised to keep us safe with Himself until death.

P We rejoice with thankful hearts that you have been baptized and have received the teaching of the Lord. You have confessed the faith and been absolved of your sins. As you continue to hear the Lord's Word and receive His blessed Sacrament, He who has begun a good work in you will bring it to completion at the day of Jesus Christ.
C **Amen.**

The catechumens kneel to receive the confirmation blessing. The pastor places his hands on the head of each catechumen and makes the sign of the cross on the forehead while saying:

P *Name*, the almighty God and Father of our Lord Jesus Christ, who has given you the new birth of water and of the Spirit and has forgiven you all your sins, strengthen you with His grace to life ☩ everlasting.
R **Amen.**

The pastor may read a text of Holy Scripture as a remembrance of confirmation.

THE LAYING ON OF HANDS

As disciples, we do not face Satan alone. Both the pastor and congregation members now express joy for God's work in our lives. At this time, the confirmand kneels in order to receive a blessing through the Word of God, which the pastor prays will strengthen the confirmand to remain in the faith. A Bible passage is often given to remind us that God promises to remain faithful to us.

Prayers

The prayers that follow express the congregation's joy at the good confession just made by the confirmands. The pastor and congregation pray for God's continued blessing upon the confirmands that they continue in the good confession just made.

After all the catechumens have received the blessing, one or both of the following collects are prayed.

Stand

P Let us pray.
Lord God, heavenly Father, we thank and praise You for Your great goodness in bringing these Your sons and daughters to the knowledge of Your Son, our Savior, Jesus Christ, and enabling them both with the heart to believe and with the mouth to confess His saving name. Grant that, bringing forth the fruits of faith, they may continue steadfast and victorious to the day when all who have fought the good fight of faith shall receive the crown of righteousness; through Jesus Christ, Your Son, our Lord, who lives and reigns with You and the Holy Spirit, one God, now and forever. (513)

C **Amen.**

P Almighty and most merciful Father, in the waters of Holy Baptism You have united Your children in the suffering and death of Your Son Jesus Christ, cleansing them by His blood. Renew in them the gift of Your Holy Spirit, that they may live in daily contrition and repentance with a faith that ever clings to their Savior. Deliver them from the power of Satan and preserve them from false and dangerous doctrines, that they may remain faithful in hearing Christ's Word and receiving His body and blood. By the Lord's Supper strengthen them to believe that no one can make satisfaction for sin but Christ alone. Enable them to find joy and comfort only in Him, learning from this Sacrament to love You and their neighbor and to bear their cross with patience and joy until the day of the resurrection of their bodies to life immortal; through Jesus Christ, Your Son, our Lord, who lives and reigns with You and the Holy Spirit, one God, now and forever. (514)

C **Amen.**

P Peace ☩ be with you.

C **Amen.**

Reception of Members by Transfer or Profession of Faith

This rite is used for receiving into membership those who were previously confirmed as Lutherans.

All gather near the font, at the chancel steps, or before the altar, as local custom dictates.

P Beloved in the Lord, our Lord Jesus Christ said to His apostles: "Whoever confesses Me before men, I will also confess before My Father who is in heaven. But whoever denies Me before men, I will also deny before My Father who is in heaven." Lift up your hearts, therefore, to the God of all grace and joyfully give answer to what I now ask you in the name of the Lord.

Matthew 10:32–33 NKJV alt.

Address to Those Desiring Membership

The rite of reception of members gives the opportunity for the newest members to confess Jesus before the congregation and therefore join in the public confession and work of the congregation.

Baptismal Question

P Do you this day in the presence of God and of this congregation acknowledge the gifts that God gave you in your Baptism?

R *Yes, I do.*

We can confess Jesus because we have received Christ's gifts in Baptism. When we were baptized, the Holy Spirit rescued us from the tyranny of Satan and placed us under the gracious care of Christ. He removed our unbelief and gave us faith. He raised us from death and gave us life. The next few questions ask us to confess this marvelous event: our rescue from Satan's realm of death and our transfer into Christ's realm of life.

Renunciation of the Devil

P Do you renounce the devil and all his works and all his ways?

R *Yes, I renounce them.*

In confessing Jesus we also renounce the devil and his former hold on us. So it was for the first disciples, and so it is for us. The rite opens with a rejection of our old master, Satan. It is a complete disavowal. We not only reject him, but we also reject his methods of deception and his works of unbelief. Nothing makes Satan angrier than when we turn our backs on him. But we now cling to One who is much stronger than Satan. In Baptism we were given a new name and live under the name of the Father, Son, and Holy Spirit.

P Do you believe in God, the Father Almighty, in Jesus Christ, His only Son our Lord, and in the Holy Spirit?

R *Yes, I believe in God the Father, Son, and Holy Spirit.*

Confession of God the Father, Son, and Holy Spirit

So, having renounced the devil, who has taken his place? To whom do we now cling? Luther suggested in his Large Catechism that we begin by answering: He is the one who "created heaven and earth!" (Large Catechism II 11). This is a way of saying that there is no other God. If God did not create everything that exists, then He is not God. My God not only created me, but He also rescued me from Satan's clutches. The story is dramatic and remarkable. The Creator became a human creature. The Son of God, our Creator, then suffered and died for us. The Spirit continues the work of Christ here on earth. Where Christ obtained salvation for us, the Spirit now delivers that salvation to us. He does so within the Church, where He keeps us safe with Christ and brings us to everlasting life through the resurrection of the body.

P Do you hold all the prophetic and apostolic Scriptures to be the inspired Word of God and the doctrine of the Evangelical Lutheran Church, drawn from them and confessed in the Small Catechism, to be faithful and true?

R *I do.*

Confession of the Teaching of the Lutheran Church

As disciples, we are not loners. We learn from others who have shared what they learned in creeds and confessions. The Apostles' Creed summarizes the faith that Christians have treasured for centuries. In a similar way, the Small Catechism summarizes the Scriptures for those new to the faith. The Large Catechism helps pastors and mature Christians to plumb the depths of Scriptures' treasures. And so here we confess that the teachings of the Lutheran Church as summarized in the catechism correspond to the Bible's witness to Christ.

Intention to Live a Faithful Life

Thus far we have renounced our former master, the devil, and with him a life of unbelief. We then confessed our faith in the triune God by confessing all that the Father, Son, and Holy Spirit have done in our lives. We now look toward the future. How will we carry out our callings as people who live under the gracious lordship of Jesus Christ?

Intention to Use the Means of Grace

The Holy Spirit made us disciples of Christ by means of the Gospel. By hearing the Word of God we enter into conversation with Christ whereby He comes and reassures us of His love and care. And that is not all. Jesus invites us to His Table with the words, "Take eat; take drink." Here He gives us His very body and blood by which He obtained the forgiveness of sins for us! By means of this meal, Christ keeps us close to Himself until He returns in glory and raises us from the dead, at which time we will enjoy an eternal banquet in the new creation.

P Do you intend to hear the Word of God and receive the Lord's Supper faithfully?

R *I do, by the grace of God.*

Intention to Live by the Word

As disciples we will face many distractions in life. We will encounter temptations to turn away from Jesus. Our lives depend upon the Word of God. It nourishes us and keeps us with Christ. To deny the Word is to reject the One who speaks to us and keeps us close to Himself. And so there is a connection between living according to the Word and living under the care of the Father, Son, and Holy Spirit.

P Do you intend to live according to the Word of God, and in faith, word, and deed to remain true to God, Father, Son, and Holy Spirit, even to death?

R *I do, by the grace of God.*

INTENTION TO REMAIN FAITHFUL TO DEATH

P Do you intend to continue steadfast in this confession and Church and to suffer all, even death, rather than fall away from it?

R *I do, by the grace of God.*

The road that Jesus chose was not an easy one. It led Him to the cross for our salvation. Jesus calls upon us as His disciples to follow Him. When we renounced Satan and confessed Christ, we entered into a battle that will continue until Christ returns in glory. Satan will use the various struggles and trials of life to raise doubts about God's goodness. He will try and seduce us into idolizing the good things in life in order to draw us away from God. God has promised to keep us safe with Himself until death.

INTENTION TO JOIN IN THE WORK OF THE CONGREGATION

P Do you desire to become a member of this congregation?

R *I do.*

P Will you support the work our gracious Lord has given this congregation with your prayers and the gifts God has given you?

R *I will, with the help of God.*

The work of a disciple is not done in isolation from the Church. The local congregation, even as it prays, "Thy kingdom come," sets about the work of the kingdom to proclaim the Good News of Jesus Christ, to faithfully confess the reason for the hope we have, and to live as a witness to God's grace.

RECEPTION AS A MEMBER

P Upon this your confession of faith, I acknowledge publicly that you are ___*a member/members*___ of the Evangelical Lutheran Church and of this congregation. Receive the Lord's Supper and participate with us in all the blessings of salvation that our Lord has given to His Church, in the name of the Father and of the ☩ Son and of the Holy Spirit.

C **Amen.**

As disciples, we do not face Satan alone. Both the pastor and the congregation members now express joy for God's work in our lives. The newest member now receives the invitation to join the congregation at the Lord's Table and participate in the congregation's service done in God's name.

Prayer

The prayer that follows expresses the congregation's joy at the good confession just made by the newest members of the congregation. The pastor and congregation pray for God's continued blessing upon them that they continue in the good confession just made.

Stand

P Let us pray.
Lord God, heavenly Father, we thank and praise You for Your great goodness in bringing these Your sons and daughters to the knowledge of Your Son, our Savior, Jesus Christ, and enabling them both with the heart to believe and with the mouth to confess His saving name. Grant that by Your Word and Spirit they may continue steadfast in the one true faith in the fellowship of this congregation as together we await the day when all who have fought the good fight of faith shall receive the crown of righteousness; through Jesus Christ, Your Son, our Lord, who lives and reigns with You and the Holy Spirit, one God, now and forever. (515)

C **Amen.**

The pastor may extend the right hand of fellowship, greeting each by name. The rite concludes with the following blessing:

P The grace of our ☩ Lord Jesus Christ be with you.

C **Amen.**

LIVING THE FAITH

INTRODUCTION

Earlier, we used the analogy of a tree to describe the life of faith. Just as a tree sinks its roots deep and wide into the ground in order to draw its nourishment, so faith sinks its roots deep into the faith, namely, it immerses itself in the story and gifts of God. Just as a tree grows tall and strong once firmly rooted, so the life of faith grows strong and vigorous when firmly rooted in the faith.

To better understand how this plays out in practice with the catechism, we might pursue our analogy with a tree a little further. Biologists will tell us that trees, like other living organisms, have a genetic code imprinted upon them. This genetic code guides the tree's life cycle. It directs the roots down and out into the soil. It guides the development of some roots for extracting nutrients and other roots for storage. It informs the tree when to bud leaves and when to drop leaves. It shapes the tree's growth. It ultimately shapes the way the tree looks when it is full grown.

In an analogous (albeit imperfect) way, the catechism provides the genetic code for the Christian life of faith. The Spirit imprints it upon us as we embrace it and learn it by heart until it becomes "second nature" for us. That is to say, the Holy Spirit's way of thinking and living becomes instinctual to us. In a sense it "reprograms" us, it reforms us according to the way God envisioned when He created and redeemed us. The knowledge the Spirit provides transforms the mind. As Paul writes, "be transformed by the renewal of your mind" (Romans 12:2). In this respect, the catechism provides a structure for the mind and heart. It goes with us wherever we go.

Just as the genetic code informs and shapes every aspect of a tree's life, the catechism does the same for the life of faith. Here we will highlight important activities of the Christian life. First, the catechism provides a structure for drawing upon the richest food that Scripture offers. Second, the catechism introduces us to the pattern of worship in which we become immersed in the story of Christ. Third, the catechism provides a pattern for prayer so that we can open our arms wide and receive all that God desires to give us. Fourth, the catechism gives us lenses that enable us to see our life experiences as God sees them.

Rooted in the Word

A tree's roots go in search of food and water within the ground. Often, the roots end up being a mirror image of the tree above ground. That is, the roots are nearly the same size below ground as the tree is above ground. That provides a good image for the Christian life of faith—the deeper and stronger the roots of faith dig into the faith, the stronger and more fruitful the tree of faith becomes above ground. Here is where the "genetic code" of the catechism helps us.

The Bible contains a lot of material. In fact, it may appear somewhat intimidating. It is legitimate to wonder where we should begin our reading and what we should look for as we read. As a summary of the Bible, the catechism guides our reading. It directs us to the central themes of the Bible. Or, to use our metaphor, it guides the roots of the tree of faith into those areas of the soil where the most important nutrients are found.

Consider the Ten Commandments. As we saw earlier, the catechism identifies the First Commandment ("You shall have no other gods") as the source and unity of the other commandments. We can see this truth in the whole of

Scripture. For example, nearly every time God punished Israel with exile at the hands of a foreign power, it was because Israel broke the First Commandment. Similarly, throughout the Minor Prophets, Israel's relationship with God is often portrayed in terms of a faithless wife and a faithful husband. The same theme continues into the New Testament. When Jesus was asked what He considered to be the most important commandment, He responded, "Love the Lord your God with all your heart and with all your soul and with all your mind" (Matthew 22:34–40, especially v. 37).

Now consider the First Article of the Creed: "I believe in God, the Father Almighty, Maker of heaven and earth." While most of our debates today center on the question of ultimate beginnings, it is worth noting that the catechism focuses on God's current and continuing care for us: "I believe that God has made me and all creatures . . . and still takes care of them." In other words, it is primarily interested in God's daily provision and protection of His human creatures.

The same can easily be said about the Bible. To be sure, Genesis 1 and John 1 open with the confession that God created all things. But for most of the Bible, God's creative activity is recounted for the purpose of strengthening our faith in His everyday care for us. Psalm 145:16 brings out these truths beautifully, especially when it concludes: "You open Your hand; You satisfy the desire of every living thing." Similarly, in the Sermon on the Mount, Jesus encourages His hearers to consider the lilies of the field and the birds of the air. Look how God cares for them! Certainly He will care for His human creatures whom He considers of far greater worth (Matthew 6:28–30).

Imagine if someone said, "In thirty seconds or less, give me the key to unlocking the significance of Jesus Christ." The Second Article of the Creed zeroes in on three things: the incarnation, death, and resurrection of Jesus. This does not mean that other things, such as His Baptism or miracles or teachings, are unimportant. It does mean, however, that they are not as central or as key for answering the questions, "Who is Jesus Christ, and why does He matter?" And this holds for the rest of Scripture as well. Consider the Gospels. Matthew, Mark, and Luke devote nearly a third of their material to the last week of Jesus' life. The Gospel of John devotes nearly half of the book to the suffering and death of Jesus. Whenever Paul speaks of Jesus, he highlights how Jesus is descended from David according to the flesh, how He suffered for our sins, and how He rose from the dead.

And then there is the Holy Spirit. We are not always sure what to make of the Spirit. Once again, the catechism provides the key to understand the Spirit's work within our lives. The Spirit brings me to Jesus and keeps me with Jesus! The Spirit's "job" is not to replace Jesus as the center of our attention. To the contrary, like a good stage manager, the Spirit keeps Jesus front and center in our lives. The catechism elegantly captures the focus of the New Testament writers on this point. Consider the role of the Spirit in moving the ministry of Jesus forward. The Spirit provided the human body for the Son of God ("conceived by the Holy Spirit"). The Spirit inaugurated Jesus into His public ministry at His Baptism. The Spirit then led Jesus into the wilderness to do battle with Satan. By the power of the Spirit, Jesus cast out demons. Jesus was raised from the dead by the power of the Spirit. The Spirit continues the work of Christ by delivering the benefits of Christ to us.

Drawing Strength from Worship

As the roots of a tree dig deeply into the soil, the roots draw upon the various nutrients and water and deliver them to the trunk, the branches, and the leaves. Like those roots, worship draws the riches of God's grace out of His Word and delivers those nutrients of the faith to us so that they might nourish and strengthen our faith for our daily walk of life. In order that we might get the most out of that nourishment, the catechism provides something of a structure or skeleton for worship. It is not by accident that nearly every component of the catechism finds its place within the worship service. And as a general rule, the order and sequence of the catechism even mirror the order and sequence of the worship service. In this regard, it provides a liturgy for the heart.

Our Divine Service generally opens with a Confession of Sins and Absolution. This pattern repeats what we find throughout the Scriptures. The people of God come before Him to confess their sins and receive His forgiveness on account of His mercy. Throughout the Old Testament, God's prophets call upon God's wayward people to repent of their sins and to turn to Him that they might live.

In confession, we hand over our sins to God. It is like saying, "Here, God, You take them. I don't want them anymore. Get them out of my sight." And in return, God removes our sins as far as the east is from the west. He buries them in the deepest part of the ocean. Unlike humans, when God buries the hatchet, He does not leave a part of the handle sticking out of the ground so that He may grab it and hurl it at us at some future date. But just as important as confessing our sins is knowing which sins we confess. Again, the catechism focuses our attention on the First Commandment and, by implication, our failure to fear, love, and trust in God above all things. In other words, it focuses our attention on the root sin of all other sins. This is what we do when we confess in worship, "I by nature am sinful and unclean." That is to say, "I by nature am unable to fear and love God."

The catechism moves on to the Apostles' Creed as a summary of the master story of God within history from the creation of the world to the consummation of all of creation, from Genesis 1 through Revelation 22. Similarly, following Confession and Absolution, the Divine Service moves to the Service of the Word, namely, readings from the Old Testament, the New Testament letters (Epistles), the Gospels, and the sermon. All of the other stories within the Bible fit within this broad outline. This allows us to see how they contribute to the central plot of God's work to reclaim creation. Thus, when we hear the Old Testament reading, the Epistle reading, and the Gospel reading, we can locate them within the master story of God's work. As the sermon expounds the texts and applies them to our lives, it often will connect the readings to the central features of the creedal outline, especially the death and resurrection of Christ. After the sermon, we speak the Creed as a way by which we tell God and one another what we have heard from the Word.

Having heard God's Word, we respond with our prayers. And so in the catechism we move from the Creed to the Lord's Prayer. In the Divine Service we move to the prayers of the congregation in which our needs and requests are brought to God. These include the general prayers as well as the specific prayers that we offer in behalf of our fellow brothers and sisters in Christ. The Lord's Prayer often is spoken after we have made the other requests. It summarizes and gathers together anything else for which we have failed to ask.

The next portion of the catechism—Baptism, Confession, and the Lord's Supper—provide the overarching structure of God's coming to us in the Divine Service. When there is a Baptism, we open the service with this sacrament. Here a baby or an adult is brought into God's family and welcomed by the congregation. The triune name is placed upon him or her. When we confess our sins and receive absolution, we live out that Baptism on a daily and weekly basis. Finally, our service often concludes with the Lord's Supper, the meal that sustains us even as it transforms our bodies in anticipation of our resurrection on the Last Day. The catechism assists us in appreciating and embracing the rich gifts that God brings to us in these Sacraments.

STRETCHING UPWARD AND OUTWARD IN PRAYER

© George Clerk / iStockphoto.com

As trees grow, they reach for the sun. With their branches and their leaves they stretch upward and outward in order to receive the life-giving energy of the sun. Through photosynthesis they use the energy of the sun to produce food from carbon dioxide and water. As Christians draw nourishment from the soil of God's Word, they open their arms and their hands to receive His gifts. The command and promise of God provide the basis and impetus for prayer. Prayer becomes the means by which faith exercises itself to receive what God has promised to give.

One of the basic activities of the Christian life is prayer. God created us in His image in part that we might have conversations with Him. Conversations are necessary for healthy relationships. And so God walked and talked with Adam in the Garden of Eden during the cool of the evening. That conversation was broken with the fall into sin. But one could say that God reopened the conversation by sending His Word into the world as a human. And so one of the most basic activities of the Christian life involves listening to God speak as He addresses us through His Word and responding to Him in prayer. Earlier we spoke about how Luther regarded the Lord's Prayer as giving us a theology of prayer as well as an outline of prayer. We also mentioned that the catechism's explanation did not provide an exhaustive treatment of prayer. The catechism focused on the essence of prayer as bringing our needs to God and asking Him for His gifts.

Luther could also speak of prayer in broader terms as well. In fact, within the Lutheran tradition we have spoken of praying the catechism. We have to bear in mind that Luther wrote the catechism in part for this purpose. In the late Middle Ages, people who could read and had a little money would purchase a little prayer book that might consist of some Bible passages, prayers, and orders for worship and devotion. These were small books that could fit in the palm of the hand and easily fit into one's pocket. Thus you could take them wherever you went. Unfortunately, many of them focused on human works as making one right with God, and many of them directed people to the saints. In 1522, Luther published his *Personal Prayer Book* as an evangelical alternative to the medieval devotional books. It contained the texts that we find in our catechism today.

Nearly two decades later, Luther's doctor asked him to provide a model for how to pray (see, they had the same questions that we do). In response, Luther wrote a little treatise to his friend Peter called "A Simple Way to Pray." (See LW 43:193–211.) In it, Luther recommended that Peter take the Ten Commandments in hand and formulate his prayers with four strands, like weaving them together in a braid. He recommended that each commandment provide an opportunity for confession, for thanksgiving, for praise, and for request. Consider the Second Commandment: "You shall not misuse the name of the Lord your God." First, we confess our lack of trust which causes us not to go to God in prayer throughout the day. Second, we give thanks that God gives us the opportunity to approach Him in prayer and access to Him as our heavenly Father. Third, we praise Him for the great works of redemption accomplished in His name. Finally, we ask Him to help us honor His name and bear it in a way that brings Him glory.

In this way you can begin to see why the catechism is considered to be a prayer book. You can purchase a small paper copy that easily fits into a pocket or purse. In this way, we can carry it wherever we go. Then, during the course of the day, during a coffee break or lunch break, we can take it out, read one commandment and explanation, or an article of the creed, or one of the petitions, and then reflect upon what it means for us. If the text had illustrations of biblical stories (as Luther's original text did), we would have an opportunity to review how the Bible story illustrates the meaning of the catechism's text. We can then offer a prayer in connection with the portion of the text we read and perhaps use Luther's four-strand approach. If we have learned the catechism by heart, we can take a few moments to work though a small portion of it. In this way, the catechism would not only instill in us the mind-set of Scripture, but keep our hearts turned to God throughout the day.

Planting and Producing New Seedlings of Faith

Healthy and vigorous trees reproduce. They produce seeds that bring forth new trees. Some of the acorns of a white oak drop to the ground where they germinate and sprout the following year. Some of the acorns are carried far distances by birds and then sprout where they are dropped. The Christian faith is like that. It gives birth to new believers. It shares the Gospel with others. Christians produce seeds; the Holy Spirit determines when and where they sprout, thereby creating new saplings, new believers.

How often have we thought to ourselves, "I would like to tell others about Christ, but I don't know where to begin or what to say"? Today, we can no longer assume either that people believe in heaven or that they want to go there. Again, the mind-set provided by the catechism provides us with a more natural way of opening up the conversation, diagnosing the problem, and sharing the Gospel.

If we follow the flow of the catechism's thought, it might seem strange to start with a discussion of the Ten Commandments. But we should consider how the

Large Catechism handles the First Commandment. It begins with the assumption that everyone has a god. That is to say, everyone has something or someone around which they organize their lives. Everyone has something to which they look for meaning and purpose in their lives. We are creatures, and as such, we are not autonomous, independent beings. In brief, we are not God. So if we begin with the assumption that people need a "god," we can begin our conversation of the Gospel by exploring what it is that people are looking for in life, or where it is that they hope to find happiness and fulfillment. From there, we can listen to hear how those "gods" may be letting the person down. After all, no creature or creaturely thing can bear the weight of our trust or provide only what God can provide. When we sense that others are somewhat disenchanted or disappointed with their god(s), we can speak of the one and only God who will not let them down and has not let them down.

At this point, one might ask, what do we say about God? This is where the story comes in. People like stories. The Gospel is the story of God's unrelenting love. It is a dramatic story. It is God's story. It is our story. So, "let me tell you the story about the God who . . ." The Creed gives us the story line that we can relate in our words. Out of sheer, unconstrained generosity, God created us, His human creatures, and gave to us this beautiful garden planet. But we were not content to be human creatures. We wanted to be more. We wanted to be like God. In that desire and pride, we ruined this beautiful garden home. We became slaves to our own desires and captives to our self-centeredness. But God did not stand idly by and watch everything "go to hell," so to speak. He sent His Son into the world to rescue His human creatures from their bondage to sin and to free His creation from its bondage to the curse of death. And so Jesus died and rose from the dead that "I might be His own and live under Him" now and forever. He continues to work today by giving us His Holy Spirit, who brings us to Jesus, keeps us with Jesus, and makes us members of a new human race that we call the Church.

Finally, as we listen closely to the person with whom we share the Gospel, and watch for reactions of surprise, disbelief, or delight, we can proceed accordingly. The catechism moves from the Creed to the Lord's Prayer. One of the first signs of the Holy Spirit's activity within a person is the heart's desire to pray. Paul says it well: "God has sent the Spirit of His Son into our hearts, crying,

'Abba! Father!' " (Galatians 4:6). And so the Third Article of the Creed, which speaks about the Holy Spirit bringing us to faith, moves into the Lord's Prayer, where we say, "Our Father in heaven." If we discern the Spirit's work within our friend, if we see in his eyes the joy that comes from the Gospel, we can ask, "Would you like to pray with me?" We need not say the Lord's Prayer specifically (though we could). It could be a prayer of thanksgiving and a request that the Holy Spirit strengthen our faith. In any event, the catechism provides us with a pattern for speaking the Gospel to others within the course of our conversations. They may ask, like the Ethiopian eunuch, What is to prevent me from being baptized? Then we can move on to the next section of the catechism and share with them what Baptism is and what it does for us!

PROVIDING SHELTER AND SHADE

Trees play vital roles within their ecosystems. A white oak provides food for hundreds of creatures, from insects to birds to other mammals. It provides shelter and shade for squirrels, cavities for woodpeckers, and resting places for other creatures that go unnoticed by us. The life of faith similarly reaches out to feed and to provide shelter for all of God's creatures. The life of faith looks to the well-being of others without even realizing it at times. Secure with God, not having to take care of ourselves, we can look toward helping others.

Many times the Ten Commandments call upon us to do things that we may not find particularly exciting, such as listening to our parents, helping our neighbors, putting the best construction on what we hear, and being content with what we have. Often we want more exciting and spectacular assignments. Luther recognized this tendency. In the Large Catechism he spoke of those who regarded the Commandments as demeaning and unexciting. Yet he reminded his readers that these are the things that God wants us to do. They describe the way His creation works. The Commandments provide protective fences around the community, individuals, and our creaturely gifts. They provide the guides that channel our energies for the benefit of God's creation and all of His creatures. Again, the First Commandment comes into play. Where we fear and trust God above all things, the rest falls into place.

The First Article of the Apostles' Creed wonderfully brings out God's ongoing work of creation and preservation. In particular, we learn here that people (us and others) function as God's instruments and tools. He created us to be His partners and co-workers in developing our garden home for the benefit of both His human and nonhuman creatures. We are sort of like the garden gloves on God's hands. And so through His nonhuman creatures He produces air, water, and the conditions necessary for life. Through His human creatures God produces food and shelter for us. Through His nonhuman creatures God raises plants, animals, and insects. Through His human creatures God produces medicines and cures from those plants, animals, and insects. So, on the one hand, that means other creatures are instruments of God's blessing to us. But, on the other hand, it also means that we are God's instruments of blessing for others that they might be fed, clothed, and sheltered as well.

In the Lord's Prayer we pray for daily bread. Among other things, we confess here that God gives daily bread even to unbelievers. What is meant by "daily bread" includes everything that we need for daily life. It includes, food, water, good friends and neighbors, good government, good weather, and the like. God keeps His world going despite human sin and thanklessness. He does so in anticipation of bringing forth His new creation from the old creation. The work that God accomplishes through us for the well-being of His creatures is for their good that they might live and enjoy God's world. Although the work that we do cannot and will not usher in a utopian society (that is Christ's and the Spirit's work), it is still important. It is God's work. That is one of the major points that the catechism sought to make in the Table of Duties (creaturely and Christian responsibilities).

Bending but Not Breaking

Trees live out in the world where they encounter all weather conditions. They endure periods of drought and flood. They face violent windstorms and thunderstorms. Their branches at times are weighed down by ice storms and snowstorms. And, yes, there are times of gentle breezes and warming sunshine. All of this is not too different from the seasons of the Christian faith. As Christians we experience times of joy over the birth of a child, the marriage of a friend, and the fruit of our labors. We also encounter times of sadness and perplexity, from illnesses to job loss to betrayal by friends to the death of family members. The catechism here, too, provides us with God's "genetic coding" that can help us cope, endure, and live in hope! In other words, we may bend beneath the weight of a fallen world, but God will not let us break.

The Ten Commandments might not seem the place to begin when we are down. After all, why kick someone when he is down? However, at times we might need something of an intervention. We might seek other gods not only when things are going well (gods such as new cars and clothes) but also when things are going badly. In those moments, we may be tempted to give up on the one true God. We might give in to despair. Yet the First Commandment stands to expect nothing but good things from God! Look to Him for all that you need! He is the only one who can help., Luther explains in the Large Catechism that even with the Second Commandment God shows us He wants to help. It is like a parent telling a child, "Ask me for help." The command highlights how earnest the parent is about wanting to help.

When we review the Creed and all that God has done and is doing from the beginning of creation to the new creation, we get a sense of God's *modus operandi* (method of working) or his SOP (standard operating procedure). He has a good track record. Everything is moving forward and being renewed as He intended. Creation continues to produce food and water and air despite everything we do to destroy it. Christ has abolished death in His dying body and brought forth the new creation in His resurrected body despite everything that sin, death, and the devil threw at Him. The Spirit is gathering the new people of God and preserving them despite everything that Satan and the unbelieving culture do to undermine the Christian faith. In this context, from eternity to eternity, we can draw comfort that God will not let us go now. He holds everything in His hands. And He is working all things out for our good and to His glory.

Luther talked about the Lord's Prayer as our weapon against tribulations and trials. It is also our comfort in which we can seek refuge. The Third Petition is particularly helpful here. In this petition, we ask that God "break and hinder" all those things that seek our demise. Note that we do not yet ask for complete deliverance from these trials (that comes in the Seventh Petition). No, here we ask that God hold them at bay so they do not get the best of us. And we ask Him to strengthen us in the face of daily problems of life. In His commentary on Psalm 23, Luther explained verse 5, "You prepare a table before me in the presence of my enemies," along these lines: With His left hand God pushes our enemies out and keeps them at arm's length. With His right hand He holds us up and strengthens us with His food. This is a very nice image to describe the Christian life of faith.

Finally, through it all, God meets us in His Sacraments. Here we find His standard operating procedure at work. God uses ordinary things to accomplish His extraordinary works. This is true whether we speak of creation, redemption, or sanctification. And so, for Luther, the Christian seeks refuge in Baptism. "I am baptized!" Against the devil, our doubts, we cling to Baptism, which snatched us from death and brought us to Christ. And every time we receive the Lord's body and blood, we know that He has not abandoned us nor forsaken us. He has given His body and blood for us and into us that we might be one with Him.

CONCLUSION

The life of faith, which draws upon the riches of the Christian faith, touches every aspect and every moment of our lives. The catechism provides us with a glimpse of the genetic code that God desired human lives to express fully in every relationship. God "programmed" it into His human creatures when He formed them from the dirt and breathed into them the breath of life. The fall into sin distorted and deformed the shape of life that God had envisioned for us. Now, through the master story of God's unceasing work on our behalf as summarized in the catechism, we have a succinct and comprehensive blueprint for us. The Spirit works actively to imprint that genetic code upon every fiber of our being. As people given the gift of faith, the Spirit works in us to express God's vision in every area of life. We do this in part by praying and practicing the catechism!

SUMMARY OF THE CHRISTIAN FAITH

The Primary Texts in Luther's Small Catechism

These are the most important texts that every Christian should learn, know, and believe.

THE TEN COMMANDMENTS

The Ten Commandments show us our sin and our need for a Savior.

You shall have no other gods.

You shall not misuse the name of the Lord your God.

Remember the Sabbath day by keeping it holy.

Honor your father and your mother.

You shall not murder.

You shall not commit adultery.

You shall not steal.

You shall not give false testimony against your neighbor.

You shall not covet your neighbor's house.

You shall not covet your neighbor's wife, or his manservant or maidservant, his ox or donkey, or anything that belongs to your neighbor. [Deuteronomy 5:6–21]

I the LORD your God am a jealous God, visiting the iniquity of the fathers on the children to the third and the fourth generation of those who hate Me, but showing steadfast love to thousands of those who love Me and keep My commandments. (Exodus 20:5–6)

THE APOSTLES' CREED

The Apostles' Creed helps us confess the God who has done everything to save us from sin through Jesus Christ and to make us members of His Church.

I believe in God, the Father Almighty, Maker of heaven and earth.

And in Jesus Christ, His only Son, our Lord, who was conceived by the Holy Spirit, born of the virgin Mary, suffered under Pontius Pilate, was crucified, died and was buried. He descended into hell. The third day He rose again from the dead. He ascended into heaven and sits at the right hand of God the Father Almighty. From thence He will come to judge the living and the dead.

I believe in the Holy Spirit, the holy Christian Church, the communion of saints, the forgiveness of sins, the resurrection of the body, and the life everlasting. Amen.

THE LORD'S PRAYER

In the Lord's Prayer we call upon God, the only source for all we need.

Our Father who art in heaven, hallowed be Thy name, Thy kingdom come, Thy will be done on earth as it is in heaven; give us this day our daily bread; and forgive us our trespasses as we forgive those who trespass against us; and lead us not into temptation, but deliver us from evil. For Thine is the kingdom and the power and the glory forever and ever. Amen. (See Matthew 6:9–13)

HOLY BAPTISM

In Holy Baptism we are united with the life, death, and resurrection of Jesus Christ. Through Baptism the Holy Spirit gives to us the forgiveness of sins, life, and salvation.

Go therefore and make disciples of all nations, baptizing them in the name of the Father and of the Son and of the Holy Spirit. (Matthew 28:19)

Whoever believes and is baptized will be saved, but whoever does not believe will be condemned. (Mark 16:16)

He saved us . . . by the washing of regeneration and renewal of the Holy Spirit, whom He poured out on us richly through Jesus Christ our Savior, so that being justified by His grace we might become heirs according to the hope of eternal life. The saying is trustworthy. (Titus 3:5–8)

We were buried therefore with Him by baptism into death, in order that, just as Christ was raised from the dead by the glory of the Father, we too might walk in newness of life. (Romans 6:4)

Confession and Absolution

Confession and Absolution daily returns us to the promises and hope given to us in our Baptism.

Jesus breathed on them and said to them, "Receive the Holy Spirit. If you forgive the sins of any, they are forgiven them; if you withhold forgiveness from any, it is withheld." (John 20:22–23)

The Lord's Supper

The Lord's Supper, also called the Sacrament of the Altar, is the true body and blood of our Lord Jesus Christ under the bread and wine, instituted by Christ Himself for us Christians to eat and to drink to strengthen faith against the temptation of the devil, the world, and our sinful flesh.

The holy evangelists Matthew, Mark, Luke, and St. Paul write:

Our Lord Jesus Christ, on the night when He was betrayed, took bread, and when He had given thanks, He broke it and gave it to the disciples and said: "Take, eat; this is My body, which is given for you. This do in remembrance of Me."

In the same way also He took the cup after supper, and when He had given thanks, He gave it to them, saying: "Drink of it, all of you; this cup is the new testament in My blood, which is shed for you for the forgiveness of sins. This do, as often as you drink it, in remembrance of Me." (Matthew 26:26–28; Mark 14:22–24; Luke 22:19–20; 1 Corinthians 11:23–25)

DEADLIEST ANIMALS

BLACK WIDOW SPIDER

A Crabtree Branches Book

Amy Culliford

Crabtree Publishing
crabtreebooks.com

School-to-Home Support for Caregivers and Teachers

This high-interest book is designed to motivate striving students with engaging topics while building fluency, vocabulary, and an interest in reading. Here are a few questions and activities to help the reader build upon his or her comprehension skills.

Before Reading:

- *What do I think this book is about?*
- *What do I know about this topic?*
- *What do I want to learn about this topic?*
- *Why am I reading this book?*

During Reading:

- *I wonder why...*
- *I'm curious to know...*
- *How is this like something I already know?*
- *What have I learned so far?*

After Reading:

- *What was the author trying to teach me?*
- *What are some details?*
- *How did the photographs and captions help me understand more?*
- *Read the book again and look for the vocabulary words.*
- *What questions do I still have?*

Extension Activities:

- *What was your favorite part of the book? Write a paragraph on it.*
- *Draw a picture of your favorite thing you learned from the book.*

TABLE OF CONTENTS

DANGEROUS SPIDERS

While most spiders pose no threat to people, some **species** can be dangerous. The black widow is one of those species. Black widow **venom** is even stronger than that of a rattlesnake.

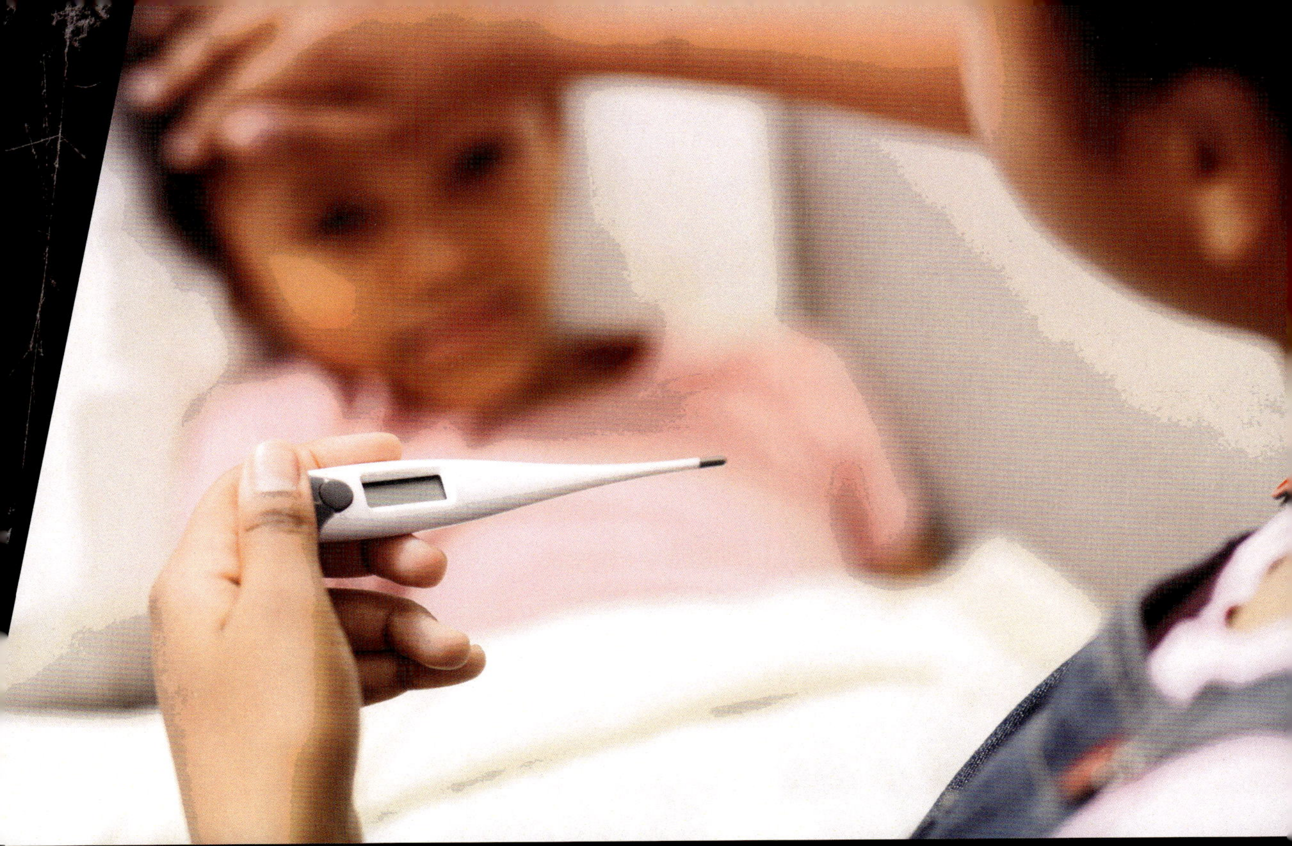

Black widow bites can cause serious symptoms for some people. Nausea, sweating, pain, and muscle aches can last for days. Only anti-venom, a type of medicine, can reduce pain and injury.

A BLACK WIDOW INJECTS LESS VENOM THAN A SNAKE. SO, A BLACK WIDOW BITE RARELY RESULTS IN DEATH.

FEAR OF SPIDERS

Arachnophobia is a big word that means fear of spiders. There are more than 40,000 species of spiders in the world. Many people fear them. However, most spiders are completely harmless to people. Spiders are actually helpful, because they **prey** on true pests like flies and mosquitoes.

Spiders use webs for many purposes, especially catching food.

SPIDERS LIVE ON EVERY CONTINENT IN THE WORLD EXCEPT ANTARCTICA.

Tarantulas, like most spiders, will only bite if they feel threatened.

WHAT'S IN A NAME?

There are over 30 kinds of black widow spiders. Their name comes from the fact that some black widow females kill and eat the male after mating. After doing so, she becomes a widow.

In the wild, female widow spiders usually do not kill their mate. However, when a pair of widow spiders are in a cage together, the female will sometimes kill the male after mating.

BLACK WIDOWS LIVE ON AVERAGE ONE TO THREE YEARS, WITH FEMALES LIVING LONGER THAN MALES.

After mating, the female builds an egg sac with her **silk**, and lays several hundred eggs inside. The **spiderlings** hatch in about ten days, and leave the sac one to two weeks later. After leaving the egg sac, the spiderlings produce a small strand of silk and are carried away with the wind.

ONLY A SMALL PERCENTAGE OF SPIDERLINGS SURVIVE TO ADULTHOOD. THAT'S BECAUSE **CANNIBALISM** IS COMMON AMONG BABY BLACK WIDOWS.

SPOTTING A BLACK WIDOW

Adult females are larger than adult males. Their bodies usually measure just under half an inch (1 cm). They are usually dark brown or shiny black. Many females have a red or orange hourglass-shaped spot on the underside of their abdomen. Some have a single triangle, or two triangles that do not connect.

Adult males are typically half the size of females. They are usually gray or black, and have red or pink spots on their backs.

The European black widow has thirteen spots on its abdomen.

BLACK WIDOW HABITAT

Black widows live in jungles, forests, deserts, and grasslands. While some spiders crawl up trees and spin webs in high places, black widows prefer to stay close to the ground. To protect themselves, they nest in dark spots among plants, rocks, and logs.

A black widow can sometimes find its way into a human home. In many cases, it is brought inside by accident. The spider may be hiding in a bunch of bananas or on a piece of firewood. Once inside, it searches for a dark, dry place to nest.

Where black widows are common, it's a good idea to shake out shoes or clothing. Any spiders hiding inside will hopefully fall out.

DEADLY WEAPONS

WEAPON 1—WEB DESIGN

Black widows are known for complex, but messy, web designs. The black widow produces different silks for different purposes.

Some silk strands are sticky. They are meant to trap prey. Other silks are smooth and are intertwined in the web. That is how the black widow can travel on her web without getting stuck.

A BLACK WIDOW HANGS UPSIDE DOWN ON HER WEB, DISPLAYING HER COLORFUL MARKINGS. SCIENTISTS BELIEVE SHE IS WARNING HER PREDATORS THAT SHE IS TOXIC.

Weapon 2—Fangs

Black widows have two sharp fangs. They come in handy when the spider wants to inject its venom.

Weapon 3—Venom

Black widow venom delivers toxins to the victim's nervous system. The toxins cause **paralysis**, and eventually death.

Did you know?
Venomous describes a dangerous fluid that is injected. **Poisonous** describes a dangerous fluid that is ingested.

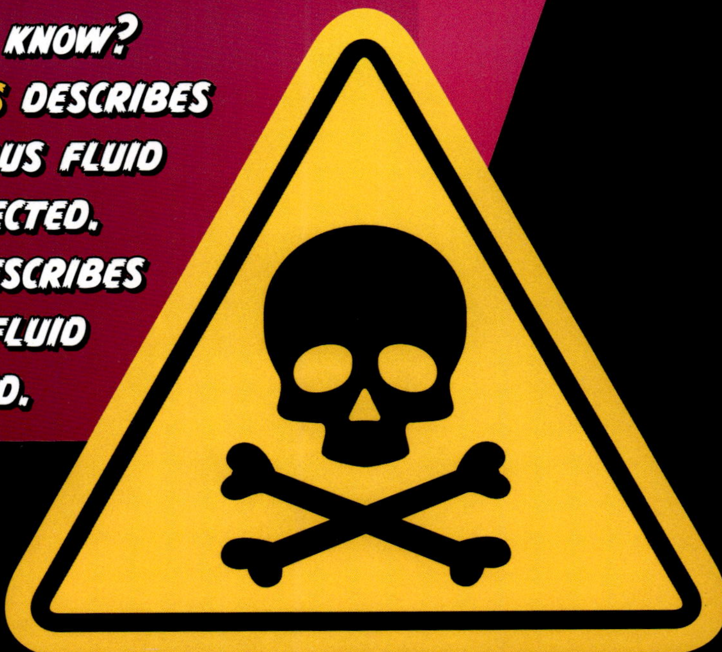

ON THE HUNT

Black widows eat bugs that get caught in their sticky web. Common foods include flies, crickets, and mosquitoes. After spinning her web, the black widow sits back and waits.

Bugs that wander too close will get trapped. When the black widow detects struggling prey, she rushes in to attack. To prevent escape, she uses silk spun from her **spinnerets** to wrap her victim tight like a mummy.

praying mantis

BLACK WIDOWS HAVE FEW **PREDATORS**. THE BLUE MUD WASP AND THE PRAYING MANTIS ARE TWO INSECTS THAT HUNT DOWN AND ENJOY A BLACK WIDOW MEAL.

Next, using her sharp fangs, the widow bites and injects a deadly dose of venom.

Black widow venom kills, but it doesn't stop there. The venom contains digestive **enzymes** that liquify the dead body. After giving the venom time to work, the black widow returns to suck up the juices.

A DANGEROUS GAME

Spider-Man is a famous comic book character. He is a young superhero who gained his super powers after being bitten by a spider. Three young brothers from Bolivia were fascinated by the Spider-Man story. One day, while working on the family farm, they spotted a black widow. Believing they could gain super powers too, the boys provoked the black widow into biting them. They got the typical pinprick bite they were hoping for.

But, the effects of the bite quickly spread throughout their bodies. They became very sick and were taken to a hospital. After more than a week of medical treatment, the boys recovered from their venomous bites.

The brothers were lucky, and survived their black widow bites. If the black widow had injected more venom the result could have been worse. Black widow venom is very potent. It can be life-threatening to small children, the elderly, and people with poor health. That's why black widows are considered one of the world's deadliest animals.

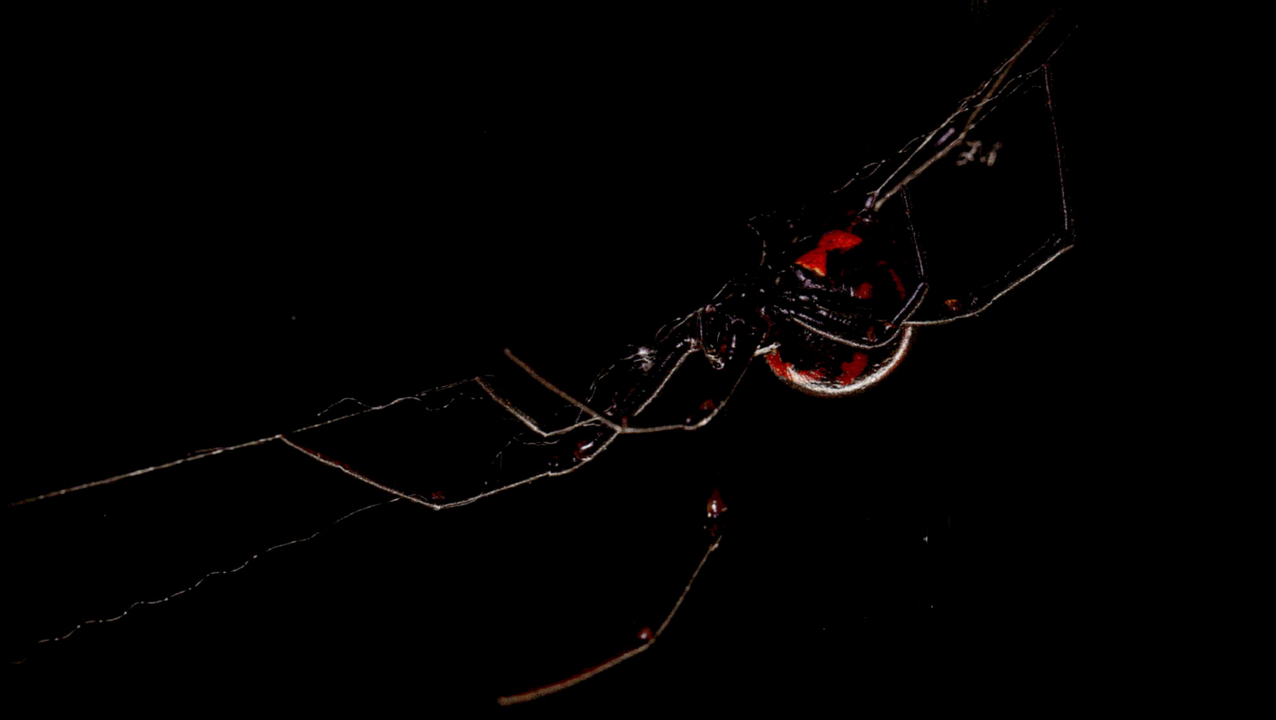

BLACK WIDOWS ARE NOT NORMALLY AGGRESSIVE TOWARD PEOPLE. GIVEN THE CHANCE, THEY WILL SCURRY AWAY RATHER THAN BITE A PERSON. THEY BECOME DANGEROUS TO PEOPLE ONLY WHEN THEY ARE THREATENED.

GLOSSARY

arachnophobia (a-RAK-nuh-FOE-bee-uh): The extreme fear of spiders

cannibalism (KAN-ih-buhl-iz-uhm): The practice of eating the flesh of one's own kind

enzymes (EN-zymz): Proteins in bodies that cause reactions

paralysis (puh-RAL-uh-siss): Inability to move or feel

predators (PRED-uh-torz): Animals that hunt and eat other animals

prey (PRAY): An animal that is hunted by another animal for food

silk (SILK): The soft, shiny, strong thread spun by an animal

species (SPEE-sheez): A certain type of animal or plant

spiderlings (SPY-dur-LINGZ): Young spiders

spinnerets (SPIN-uh-rets): Organs in which silk is produced

toxic (TOK-sik): Harmful

venom (VEN-uhm): Harmful fluid delivered by injection

Index

Websites to Visit

https://kids.nationalgeographic.com/animals/invertebrates/black-widow/

www.ducksters.com/animals/black_widow_spider.php

About the Author

Amy Culliford

Amy Culliford has a Bachelor of Fine Arts. She has worked as a classroom drama teacher and led after-school drama programs. She avoids spiders of any kind.

The author would like to thank David and Patricia Armentrout for their research and help on this project.

Crabtree Publishing

crabtreebooks.com 800-387-7650

Produced by: Blue Door Education for Crabtree Publishing
Written by: Amy Culliford
Designed by: Jennifer Dydyk
Edited by: Tracy Nelson Maurer
Proofreader: Crystal Sikkens

Hardcover	978-1-4271-5412-5
Paperback	978-1-4271-5418-7
Ebook (pdf)	978-1-4271-5424-8
Epub	978-1-4271-5430-9
Read-along	978-1-4271-5436-1
Audio book	978-1-4271-5442-2

Printed in Canada/062024/CPC20240614

Published in Canada
Crabtree Publishing
616 Welland Avenue
St. Catharines, Ontario
L2M 5V6

Published in the United States
Crabtree Publishing
347 Fifth Avenue
Suite 1402-145
New York, NY 10016

Photographs: Cover photo © lighTTrace Studio, graphic splat on cover and throughout © Andrii Symonenko /Shutterstock.com, page 4, 8, 9, 14, 15, 18, 19, 20, 21, 28, 29 web background © maxshutter/istockphoto.com, spider © BVDC/istockphoto.com, page 5 © Prostock-Studio/istockphoto.com, pages 6, 7, 10, 11, 12, 13, 16, 17, 22, 23 web background © RAYOCLICKS/istockphoto.com, page 6 spider © Holly Guerrio/istockphoto.com, page 7 map © lukbar/istockphoto.com, tarantula © yew/istockphoto.com, page 8 and 29 spider © Mainely Photos/istockphoto.com, page 9 spiders © Frank Buchter/istockphoto.com, page 10 spider and ll spiderlings © Frank Buchter/istockphoto.com, page 12 spiders © Mark Kostich/istockphoto.com, page 13 spider © Frank Buchter/istockphoto.com, page 14 bottom photo © EstherCristina/istockphoto.com, page 15 rainforest (top) © miroslav_1/istockphoto.com, cactus © lucky-photographer/istockphoto.com, flowers © Jesse Walker/istockphoto.com, trees © Alexander Fattal/istockphoto.com, page 16 spider © Richard Par/istockphoto.com, page 17 spider © Jeffrey Schreier/istockphoto.com, page 18 spider © Muratani/istockphoto.com, page 19 (top) © Eleasha Strickland/istockphoto.com, (bottom © Robert Meyer/istockphoto.com, page 20 spider © MediaProduction/istockphoto.com, page 21 yellow sign © Ondřej Pros/istockphoto.com, page 22 spider © ArmanDavtyan/istockphoto.com, page 23 (top) © Hcirdoog| Dreamstime.com, (bottom) © aetmeister/istockphoto.com, pages 24-25 © Therina Groenewald| Dreamstime.com, page 26 spiderman © Editorial credit: Thoranin Nokyoo / Shutterstock.com, page 27 © jamesdvdsn/istockphoto.com, page 28 spider © AmericanWildlife/istockphoto.com

Library and Archives Canada Cataloguing in Publication

Title: Black widow spider / Amy Culliford.
Names: Culliford, Amy, 1992- author.
Description: Series statement: Deadliest animals |
"A Crabtree branches book". | Includes index.
Identifiers: Canadiana (print) 20210218878 |
Canadiana (ebook) 20210218886 |
ISBN 9781427154125 (hardcover) |
ISBN 9781427154187 (softcover) |
ISBN 9781427154248 (HTML) |
ISBN 9781427154309 (EPUB) |
ISBN 9781427154361 (read-along ebook)
Subjects: LCSH: Black widow spider—Juvenile literature.
Classification: LCC QL458.42.T54 C85 2022 | DDC j595.4/4—dc23

Library of Congress Cataloging-in-Publication Data

Names: Culliford, Amy, 1992- author.
Title: Black widow spider / Amy Culliford.
Description: New York, NY : Crabtree Publishing, [2022] | Series:
Deadliest animals - a Crabtree branches book | Includes index.
Identifiers: LCCN 2021021929 (print) | LCCN 2021021930 (ebook) |
ISBN 9781427154125 (hardcover) |
ISBN 9781427154187 (paperback) |
ISBN 9781427154248 (ebook) |
ISBN 9781427154309 (epub) |
ISBN 9781427154361
Subjects: LCSH: Black widow spider--Juvenile literature. |
Dangerous animals--Juvenile literature.
Classification: LCC QL458.42.T54 C85 2022 (print) |
LCC QL458.42.T54 (ebook) | DDC 595.4/4--dc23
LC record available at https://lccn.loc.gov/2021021929
LC ebook record available at https://lccn.loc.gov/2021021930